On the Road Again
The Best Years of Our Lives
Cradle to the Grave

/

Seren Drama

LAURENCE ALLAN

On the Road Again
The Best Years of Our Lives
Cradle to the Grave

seren

seren
is the book imprint of
Poetry Wales Press Ltd
Wyndham Street, Bridgend, Wales

ISBN 1-85411-265-1

A CIP record for this title is available from
the British Library

*The publisher works with the financial assistance of the
Arts Council of Wales*

Cover Design: Andy Dark

Printed in Palatino by
WBC Book Manufacturers, Bridgend

Contents

On The Road Again

On The Road Again was first performed by Hijinx Theatre on Tuesday, April 12th, 1994 at Newport Gateway Club in Newport, Gwent, with the following cast:

RICH	Richard Berry
BEEFY	Beefy Jenkins
Directed by	Jamie Garven
Design Consultant	Jane Linz Roberts
Lighting Design &	
Stage Management	Heather Brown
Set Constructed by	Peter Furness

Characters originated from workshops with Hijinx Theatre (Richard Berry, Beefy Jenkins, Jamie Garven, Laurence Allan).

Act One

(We see the space where the two men live. There's no-one there but we see signs of a thin life. There is a fold-up camper table; on it is a radio tuned to Radio 2, a record player, and books. There is a shopping trolley clearly doubling as both larder and wardrobe. Near the perimeter of the space is a dog bowl and an unopened letter. The radio fades to a cackle. RICH appears outside the space. He is dressed for outdoors and carrying two shopping bags. RICH steps in. He picks up the dog bowl and the letter and reads)

RICH: Beefy.

(He studies the letter at length before placing it, unopened, on the table. He looks at the dog bowl lovingly before replacing it on the floor.)

RICH: Bob.

(He fiddles with the radio, to no avail.)

Batteries.

(looks at the letter)

Beefy.

(back to the dog bowl)

Bob.

(then, desperately mixing the three...)

Beefy. Batteries. Bob. Beefy. Bob. Batteries.

(He goes over to the records, chooses one, places it on

the player. We hear 'Down Town' by Petula Clark. He takes off his coat, visibly relaxing, and walks over to perimeter of space, then he looks down and beyond.)

RICH: It's good to look down over the city. Beyond the houses, where the road meets the trees, where the trees meet the sand, where the sand meets the sky. Window on the world. (*looks down to the bowl*) Bob. (*then back to the table*) Batteries. Beefy. (*plunges into one of his bags, brings out an old answering machine*) Binatone. (*flicks a switch*) Technology.

(He puts it back in the bag, then into the trolley, empties the rest of his bags, including some plastic cups and a cheap bottle of squash which he places on the table. He resists the temptation to pick up the letter.)

RICH: Good to be prepared. For the unexpected. The unexpected guest dropping by. The old chum, distant cousin, workmate. They'll always get a welcome here, this port in a storm, this happy haven, the sceptred isle, this... (*He grabs the letter.*) What is this letter? (*He studies the address on the envelope, places it back on the table, circles it, stalks it, picks it up again and holds it up to the light, then puts it down again resolutely.*)

RICH: Beefy. Batteries. Bob. Bollocks. (*rips open the letter, reads it*) Shouldn't have done that. Slight error of judgement. (*He is at a loss what to do with it, and finally stuffs it into his pocket.*) Junk, junk mail, that's all there ever is. Junk mail, junk food, junk music, there's no escaping it. (*He puts 'Down Town' back on the record player and walks to the window.*)

Think I might stroll to the sea later. Take in the ozone.

(There is a surge of music, 'Jumpin' Jack Flash' by the Rolling Stones, and BEEFY appears outside. He is

dressed in biker gear. RICH immediately plunges into a book as BEEFY approaches. The moment he enters, the music stops and we hear 'Down Town'. BEEFY stares at the record player and takes the needle off. RICH continues to whistle the tune. BEEFY tries to turn the radio on.)

BEEFY: What's wrong with this?

RICH: Good day?

BEEFY: What's wrong with this radio?

RICH: It's a beautiful evening.

BEEFY: You left it on, didn't you? Playing to itself till it clapped out.

RICH: I like to come home to the sounds of life.

BEEFY: So do I, but I have to make do with you.

           (They sit, watch and wait.)

BEEFY: Where's that letter?

RICH: What letter?

BEEFY: The letter that came this morning.

RICH: No letter came here this morning.

BEEFY: I saw a man bring it here when I was leaving.

RICH: Wasn't here, it must have been somewhere else.

BEEFY: There isn't anywhere else.

RICH: Then you must have been seeing things.

BEEFY: I do not see things.

RICH: Then perhaps you were still drunk.

BEEFY: Was not.

RICH: Blind drunk.

BEEFY: Never.

RICH: Hungover.

BEEFY: I was not.

RICH: Out of your tiny skull.

BEEFY: Was not.

RICH: Pissed as a fart.

          (*They weigh each other up, then let it go.*)

BEEFY: Four cups.

RICH: Guests.

BEEFY: What guests?

RICH: Unexpected guests.

BEEFY: Who's that then? Who are we not expecting? Cardiff City Football team? The South Wales Drug Squad? The chorus of the Welsh National Opera? Exactly who are we expecting to turn up unexpectedly?

RICH: Friends.

BEEFY: Friends! There's more chance of that flaming dog turning up.

RICH: You loved that dog.

BEEFY: I hated that dog.

          (*There is a silence between them.*)

BEEFY: Well, come on then, what have you got to show?

RICH: You go first

BEEFY: No, you go first.

RICH: Yes. Well, you've seen the cups. And the squash — diet. And I've collected some miscellaneous to add to the... (*points to the trolley*) miscellaneous.

BEEFY: Anything else?

RICH: Work? You mean work? No work today, no. But

contacts, I've made vital contacts.

BEEFY: What?

RICH: I'm meeting a man from the motor trade, waiting to keep the appointment I made. Remember that? The Beatles. We used to sing that. (*starts to sing it*)

BEEFY: No, I don't remember it and you haven't got no meeting neither.

RICH: No. But there was a job, on the forecourt of the Action Garage. But I missed it.

BEEFY: So you've got nothing to show, nothing at all. Not even a letter.

RICH: No. Yes, yes, I have got something to show you, something that will blow your socks right out of your boots.

BEEFY: I can't wait.

RICH: And neither shall you. (*He presents him with the answering machine.*) Cast your eyes on that Beefy, that is the answer to our dreams, the key to the world.

BEEFY: It's an answering machine.

RICH: Binatone.

(*They stare at it.*)

BEEFY: So?

RICH: Freedom, Beefy, Freedom. We can be out all day, while back here in Mission Control, the jobs are piling up for us.

BEEFY: What jobs?

RICH: The jobs that we do, the jobs that no-one else will do.

BEEFY: Like what?

RICH: Like what we do, like entertaining people,

making people laugh, cleaning leaves out of their gutters, sweeping forecourts of Action Garages. We can form a company now we've got that.

BEEFY: Give ourselves a name.

RICH: Yeah.

BEEFY: Yeah, like the completely useless company.

RICH: No.

BEEFY: 'Cos that's what you are, completely fucking useless.

RICH: But we've got the answering machine now.

BEEFY: Yes Rich, but we haven't got a phone, have we?

RICH: What?

BEEFY: A phone.

RICH: No. Not yet.

BEEFY: And we never will while we're living in this poxy caravan.

RICH: Mobile residence.

BEEFY: It's a shack.

RICH: It's our home.

BEEFY: Even the dog won't live in it. (*kicks the bowl again*)

RICH: Could be an office.

BEEFY: It will never make a chicken shed, not in a million years.

(*They stay moodily apart.*)

RICH: What about you? What have you been doing?

BEEFY: Doing what I do. Ducking and diving, scratching and sniffing. Doing what I do.

RICH: So what have you got to show? You had one pound forty this morning.

BEEFY: A man's got to live.

RICH: And that was for both of us, how do I live pray tell?

BEEFY: Don't ask me, you're the bollock brain with the Binatone, ask that.

RICH: I know what you've been doing.

BEEFY: I been doing what I do.

RICH: Yes, and I know what you do.

BEEFY: Do you?

RICH: Yes, I do.

(*BEEFY tries to ignore him as RICH begins an extravagant mime of someone apparently reading up a wall.*)

BEEFY: I have not been in Howells watching girls go up the escalator. I don't do that anymore.

(*RICH continues pretending to pay someone at a counter, then goes on to mime a man in a betting shop, watching the race on TV, losing, etc.*)

BEEFY: Finished?

RICH: No.

(*He goes on and imitates a man scrounging in bins, finding bottles, sitting on bench, drinking, gesticulating wildly, falling over, being abusive to people, crawling home. RICH finishes with a flourish of vomiting.*)

RICH: Remind you of anyone?

BEEFY: The Queen Mother on Ladies Day at Ascot.

RICH: It was you this afternoon in the bookies, in the bins, and then falling over in the park.

BEEFY: It was not.

RICH: Yes it was. You bet, you booze and you look up

15

women's skirts on the escalator in Howells.

BEEFY: You can't see up women's skirts on the escalator. You have to stand in the doorway between the cosmetic counter and the men's — I don't do it anyway.

RICH: But you do the rest. You're a gambler and a boozer. You're disgusting.

BEEFY: It's in my blood.

RICH: What is? British Sherry.

BEEFY: No. (*pause*) Horses.

RICH: You've never smelt a horse.

BEEFY: My father was a jockey.

RICH: Was not.

BEEFY: My grandfather was a jockey.

RICH: Liar.

BEEFY: I could have been a jockey.

RICH: Never.

BEEFY: How would you know?

RICH: You've never been near a horse.

BEEFY: Never been near a horse? Where do we always head for?

RICH: Home.

BEEFY: We go where the horses go.

RICH: Do we?

BEEFY: Redcar, what's in Redcar?

RICH: Nothing.

BEEFY: Horses. Doncaster, what about Doncaster?

RICH: They arrested you in Doncaster. You spent three

	days in the police station. Left me by myself.
BEEFY:	York then, what was in York?
RICH:	You fell in the canal in York.
BEEFY:	I did not fall, that bloody dog pushed me.
RICH:	Bob. He was a dog.
BEEFY:	Chepstow. Why were we in Chepstow?
RICH:	There was that woman in Chepstow, that woman you liked. She had gold teeth, six kids and a moped. She got us into a lot of trouble, that woman you liked.
BEEFY:	I did not like any woman in Chepstow.
RICH:	You did and she had a moped.
BEEFY:	I didn't and it wasn't a moped, it was a Bantam.
RICH:	See.
BEEFY:	Bloody hell Rich, it was the horses, we went to Chepstow because of the horses. We went everywhere because of the horses: Redcar, Doncaster, York, Chepstow. They all had racetracks with horses. Nottingham, Leicester, Uttoxeter, Cheltenham. Everywhere we went had horses.
RICH:	What about Rhyl? Rhyl didn't have horses. Donkeys, but no horses.
BEEFY:	Mostly then! Mostly we followed the horses.
RICH:	You did.
BEEFY:	Exactly, that's what I'm saying. I knew horses, and we followed the horses. I could have been a jockey, could have been a contender.
RICH:	That was boxing, Marvin Brando, *On The Waterfront*.
BEEFY:	That was a film. This is life I'm talking about,

17

what I could have done with it. Could have been a jockey. Like my father, my grandfather, my great grandfather. Come from a long line of jockeys.

(*He recites as a poem:*)

And I could have been there Riding high.
Short in the saddle.
Light and tight, like a monkey on a bear.
On the gallops, on the flat.
Epsom, Cheltenham, the 2000 Guineas.
Nijinsky, Shergar, whipping 'em home.
Or big and beefy, over the sticks.
Red Rum, Arkle, driving 'em hard.
Beechers, the Chair, I could have beaten them all.
Bare-backed, short-arsed, the four foot cowboy.
I could have been up there, with the wind and the sun and the road in my face.
Rider on the storm. Ghost rider in the sky.

RICH: What a load of tosh. So? Why aren't you a jockey in the Derby?

BEEFY: Can't all be jockeys in the Derby.

RICH: But you're not a jockey anywhere, are you? You don't ride horses, you just bet on 'em.

BEEFY: I never had the chance, did I? I was cheated.

RICH: That's not what I heard, Beefy.

BEEFY: You heard nothing. (*Silence.*) You couldn't have.

RICH: I heard you cheated.

BEEFY: Never.

RICH: You threw a race.

BEEFY: Never ever.

RICH: Lost a race deliberately.

BEEFY: I never would.

18

RICH: You did, you took the money, you cheated.

BEEFY: You are a liar.

RICH: And you are a cheat.

BEEFY: I have never cheated.

RICH: You're always cheating.

BEEFY: When? How?

RICH: You cheat on money, you cheat on women, and you cheat on me.

BEEFY: And you're always lying.

RICH: That is a lie, I never lie.

BEEFY: You're lying now.

RICH: I am certainly not.

BEEFY: See, you don't know you're doing it because you're always doing it. You lied about that woman.

RICH: That woman you fancied?

BEEFY: I did not, you made it up. Like you make this place up.

RICH: I did not make this place up.

BEEFY: Where are we then, Rich?

           (*RICH wanders to the window, gazes out.*)

RICH: Splow.

BEEFY: Splow? How do you spell that?

RICH: I don't know, I've never seen it written down.

BEEFY: Well I have and it's written Splott, S P L O T T, Splott.

RICH: How would you know? You can't even read.

BEEFY: But I know where we are, in a dirty caravan, a

splot on the landscape.

(*RICH gazes down and beyond again.*)

RICH: A splot is in the eye of the beholder.

(*Defeated, he searches for a change of tack, finds the dog bowl and clutches at it for comfort.*)

RICH: Bob. He was a dog, a clown amongst dogs.

BEEFY: He was a mutt, a monster amongst mutts.

RICH: You loved that dog.

BEEFY: I hated that dog.

RICH: He loved you.

BEEFY: He hated me, he pushed me into the canal.

RICH: He was playing.

BEEFY: He's not even ours. We only ever see his bowl. Well that can go as well. (*makes a grab for the bowl*)

RICH: I don't lie about him though. They're just stories.

BEEFY: Same difference. The woman, the dog, this caravan, you lie about them. And that letter, you're lying about that too.

RICH: What letter? You couldn't have read it even if there was a letter. I'd have to read it to you.

BEEFY: I wouldn't want to be read to by no liar.

RICH: And I wouldn't want to read to no cheat.

BEEFY: Right.

RICH: Right.

BEEFY: I don't know what I'm doing living with a liar.

RICH: And I don't know what I'm doing living with a cheat.

BEEFY: All this time tramping around with a liar.

RICH: I didn't tramp, I wandered.

BEEFY: And lied.

RICH: While you cheated. With your bookies and your horses. How did I put up with it?

BEEFY: Well you won't have to anymore, will you?

RICH: No, I won't.

BEEFY: Because that is it.

RICH: It certainly is.

BEEFY: The end of the road.

RICH: The end of the road.

(*They spend some time weighing this up.*)

RICH: How do you mean the end of the road?

BEEFY: I mean we have reached the end of the road.

RICH: Well yes, I know. This is the end of the road. Home.

BEEFY: Not my home Rich, yours. And me and you are no more.

RICH: No more?

BEEFY: Finito.

RICH: I thought you meant you were going to stop cheating.

BEEFY: And you stop lying?

RICH: I don't lie.

BEEFY: See. It's no good, mun. It's the end of the road. Over.

RICH: But we've got a place here, we've never had a place before.

BEEFY: It's not a place, it's a splot. And I don't belong in no splot.

RICH: But it's somewhere, and everyone's got to be somewhere.

BEEFY: No they don't. Some people like to be anywhere. And that's where I want to be. Anywhere.

RICH: Except here.

BEEFY: I been here. And now I'm going.

RICH: By yourself?

BEEFY: By myself.

(*RICH stares at him. BEEFY stares out of the window.*)

BEEFY: I don't know what I'm doing here anyway. Look at it, not a horse in sight. (*RICH joins him.*)

RICH: There's the bookies, the turf accountant. That's horses.

(*BEEFY moves back to the table and picks up the radio.*)

BEEFY: This is my radio, you know. And you've wasted the batteries.

RICH: Look, Beefy. What I said about cheating, it doesn't matter.

BEEFY: I doesn't matter that I'm a cheat?

RICH: No.

BEEFY: But I am a cheat?

RICH: Cheats and liars, they're two of a kind, aren't they? They go together.

BEEFY: Am I cheat?

RICH: No.

BEEFY: You liar.

RICH: I'm not. I don't think you're a cheat, Beefy. You're not a cheat. You just like to look at life differently.

You like to bend life.

BEEFY: Like you bend the truth.

RICH: Yes, yes that's it. I'm a truthbender and you're a lifebender. That's us, creators of our universe. (*He looks out and beyond his window. BEEFY finds a bag and shoves the radio into it.*)

BEEFY: Creators be buggered. Prisoners we are Rich, and I'm off, over the wall.

(*He rummages through the trolley.*)

RICH: You don't have to go now. We've sorted it, haven't we, got it out into the open. We know who we are now.

BEEFY: And it's no use, is it? You're no good for me, I'm no good for you. You want to stay, I want to go. Simple as that.

RICH: Simple as that. (*He gazes out of the window.*) What if I said I wanted to go as well?

BEEFY: I'd say you were lying.

RICH: I'm not.

BEEFY: You are.

RICH: I'm not.

BEEFY: Well, do you?

RICH: No.

BEEFY: There.

RICH: No, I don't want to go. I don't want to follow the horses anymore. I want to stay here.

BEEFY: Well, there we are then.

RICH: There we are then.

(*BEEFY carries on a random pack.*)

RICH: Sorry about the batteries.

BEEFY: Forget it.

RICH: I'll try and send some on.

BEEFY: Forget it.

RICH: It's not really yours, you know.

BEEFY: What?

RICH: The radio. It's not really yours.

BEEFY: It is mine, I won it playing cards.

RICH: You cheated. So it's not really yours.

BEEFY: I did not cheat.

RICH: You did. I saw you cheating.

BEEFY: You liar! I never cheat at cards, never.

RICH: You always cheat at cards. It's the only way you know how to play.

BEEFY: Liar.

RICH: Cheat.

BEEFY: Liar.

RICH: Lifebender.

BEEFY: (*stops himself short*) Have it then. Keep the damn thing.

RICH: I'm not saying it's mine. You won it from that seafaring fellow in Bristol. He could be anywhere. Anywhere out there on the ocean.

BEEFY: Seafaring. He had a yellow plastic mac, that's all.

RICH: He had salt in his blood, that man. And that's his radio.

(*BEEFY empties his bag back into the trolley.*)

BEEFY: What about this lot, then? Any of this yours? I wouldn't want to cheat you out of your rightful property.

RICH: I don't know. Some of it's yours, some of it's mine, but most of it's ours. I mean, that's our life in that trolley.

BEEFY: It's a Tesco trolley full of junk.

RICH: No, no. That's our life's rich tapestry in there. A chart of our incredible journey.

(*He takes out a builder's hard hat and puts it on.*)

What does that say to you?

BEEFY: Pratt.

RICH: Security guard.

(*He holds out a blackened piece of bar.*)

From our antique collection.

BEEFY: Scrap.

RICH: It's worth money.

BEEFY: It's scrap, we used it as a poker.

RICH: Did we?

BEEFY: Yes.

RICH: A poker?

BEEFY: When we had a fire.

RICH: When we slept out. It never did the job.

BEEFY: Useless.

RICH: It did have it's uses. Remember?

BEEFY: No.

RICH: You do.

BEEFY: I don't.

RICH: You do.

BEEFY: Alright! I remember. (*pause*)

RICH: Bullies.

BEEFY: Rednecks.

RICH: Bigots.

BEEFY: Bastards.

RICH: Big bastards.

BEEFY: Big bastard bastards.

RICH: Bastard big bastard bastards.

BEEFY: Bastard, bastard big bastard bastards.

RICH: Got you arrested.

BEEFY: Fourteen days.

RICH: By myself.

BEEFY: I never touched him.

RICH: Scraped his nose.

BEEFY: Should have bust his lip.

RICH: There were four of them.

BEEFY: Built like ships.

RICH: Bigger than us.

BEEFY: They always are.

RICH: They always are.

BEEFY: And where were you?

RICH: I was —

BEEFY: Where?

RICH: I was —

BEEFY: Yeah?

RICH: I was —

            (*BEEFY lets him hang.*)

BEEFY: Useless.

RICH: You better keep that then. (*hands him the poker*)

BEEFY: Aye. For the fire.

RICH: For the fire.

          (*RICH takes out a lump of coal.*)

RICH: What about this, then? Coal for the fire.

BEEFY: No.

RICH: No?

BEEFY: You'd burn that?

RICH: No.

BEEFY: Why not?

RICH: Haven't got a fire.

          (*BEEFY grabs the coal from him.*)

BEEFY: Yorkshire.

RICH: In England.

BEEFY: Doncaster.

RICH: The strike.

BEEFY: Six months.

RICH: Picking coal.

BEEFY: With bare hands.

RICH: Blood and blisters.

BEEFY: You were too soft.

RICH: Wasn't.

BEEFY: You wanted to sell it.

RICH: Didn't.

BEEFY: Did.

RICH: Couldn't.

BEEFY: Wouldn't.

RICH: You were too soft.

BEEFY: We gave it away.

RICH: And they gave us sandwiches. Chicken sand-
           wiches.

BEEFY: Corned beef.

RICH: Asparagus soup.

BEEFY: Oxtail.

RICH: And peaches and cream.

BEEFY: Pineapple chunks.

RICH: You were arrested.

BEEFY: One night and a porridge.

RICH: You were let off.

BEEFY: I wanted to stay.

RICH: They weren't our jobs.

BEEFY: No bugger's now.

RICH: We would have made good miners.

BEEFY: Too old.

RICH: Too short.

BEEFY: Too late.

           (*RICH goes to give him the coal.*)

BEEFY: No, you have that. (*pause*) Corned beef.

RICH: Oxtail soup.

BOTH: And pineapple chunks.

           (*RICH takes out a penny whistle.*)

RICH: Look.

BEEFY: I thought we'd chucked that.

RICH: I wouldn't do that. This is the very thing people remember us by. They'll look back and they'll say, "One played." (*He gestures to BEEFY.*)

BEEFY: Who shouldn't.

RICH: "And one sang."

BEEFY: Who couldn't.

RICH: This made people laugh.

BEEFY: It wasn't meant to though, was it? I put my heart and soul into that.

RICH: And they laughed.

BEEFY: Yes. And why did they laugh? Because you were dancing, that's why. There's me playing my guts out while you ponced about like a drug-crazed morris dancer.

RICH: I never danced.

BEEFY: Don't start that.

RICH: I never danced. Bob danced.

BEEFY: Bob! Don't be so dull, who ever heard of a dancing dog?

RICH: They're very common in France.

BEEFY: But very rare in Doncaster.

RICH: Except for Bob. A dancer amongst dogs, he was: the tango...

BEEFY: He never danced.

RICH: ...the boogalloo twist...

BEEFY: He never danced.

RICH: ...the pony...

BEEFY: He never danced.

29

RICH: ...the foxtrot.

BEEFY: That dog never danced. He hopped about a bit when I booted him up the —

RICH: That was a vicious, unprovoked act.

BEEFY: He was rogering my leg.

RICH: He was playing.

BEEFY: Playing! He hated me and I hated him.

RICH: That is a wicked thing to say about our dog. He loved you.

BEEFY: Listen, that is not our dog. He can't dance and I definitely hated him.

            (*Silence.*)

RICH: I never danced.

BEEFY: Don't start.

RICH: But I didn't.

BEEFY: You did.

            (*Silence.*)

RICH: I sang.

BEEFY: I know.

RICH: You played.

BEEFY: I know.

RICH: Here's one I used to sing on my mother's knee — and other low joints. That's the joke I used to start us off with, remember?

BEEFY: I remember.

RICH: And nobody laughed. Ever.

BEEFY: Ever.

RICH: They laughed at you playing.

BEEFY: They laughed at you dancing.

           (*RICH hands him the penny whistle.*)

RICH: Play us something now.

BEEFY: So you can laugh.

RICH: No, I won't laugh. I'll sing.

BEEFY: You going to introduce it with that joke?

RICH: No, no jokes.

BEEFY: And no dancing.

RICH: Definitely no dancing. Serious.

BEEFY: Serious?

RICH: Deadly.

BEEFY: I used to be good at this.

RICH: You did.

BEEFY: And you used to spoil it.

RICH: I... I won't. I won't this time.

           (*BEEFY plays and RICH sings. "You've Got To Hide Your Love Away".*)

RICH: See, no one laughed.

BEEFY: That's because you didn't dance.

RICH: It was good, wasn't it?

BEEFY: Better than cleaning leaves out of gutters.

RICH: Why did we stop?

BEEFY: You tell me.

RICH: I don't know.

BEEFY: You don't remember?

RICH: I certainly don't.

BEEFY: Rich, you were arrested.

RICH: I certainly was not.

BEEFY: They arrested you because you were dancing like a tart, disturbing the peace. They carted you off to clink.

RICH: That is an outrageous slur. I have never been arrested in my life.

BEEFY: They had you handcuffed in the back of a black Maria.

RICH: It was a misunderstanding. I was trying to control Bob, he was having a fit.

BEEFY: You spent a night in the cells.

RICH: Never. I was released as soon as they realised their mistake.

BEEFY: And we have never played since.

RICH: You can't blame me.

BEEFY: You ruined it all.

RICH: You are the troublemaker.

BEEFY: Same as you butt, whether you like it or not.

RICH: It's a slur and a lie. (*kicks the dog bowl*) It was that fucking dog's fault anyway.

             (*Long silence. BEEFY starts to go.*)

RICH: Yes, you keep the whistle. And you've got your poker.

             (*BEEFY is going.*)

RICH: What about the hat? Could come in handy.

BEEFY: No. You were the security guard.

             (*RICH starts lifting things out of the trolley. They are old and broken, e.g. a paintbrush.*)

BEEFY: And you were the painter.

(*plunger*)

Plumber.

(*tin of nails*)

You were also the carpenter.

(*a stick*)

Shepherd.

(*rubber arms bands*)

Lifeguard.

(*brush*)

Chimney sweep.

(*another brush*)

Toilet attendant.

BEEFY: You've lived, haven't you Rich?

RICH: You can have the coal if you like.

BEEFY: No, ta.

RICH: And you don't want the hat.

BEEFY: No.

RICH: The radio, take the radio.

BEEFY: No batteries.

(*RICH throws everything down. BEEFY starts to go.*)

RICH: What about the books? (*RICH gets the book out with absolute desperation.*) You'd forgotten about the books.

(*BEEFY stops in his tracks.*)

BEEFY: Aye, I'd forgotten about the books.

RICH: They're yours as well.

BEEFY: Yeah, I enjoyed those books.

RICH: Of an evening.

BEEFY: Before we had a radio.

RICH: That I always wore out.

          (*BEEFY picks one up.*)

BEEFY: What's that one?

RICH: *Great Expectations.*

BEEFY: Magwitch.

RICH: Pip old chap.

BEEFY: Saw the film in Pontypridd when I was a boy.

RICH: When films were pictures.

BEEFY: Magwitch. Scared the daylights out of me.

RICH: Black and white.

BEEFY: Big, bald convict, wanne?

RICH: Hiding in the cemetery.

BEEFY: Cold and starvated.

RICH: Dark and misten.

BEEFY: On the run.

RICH: And along happens Pip.

BEEFY: Out he pounces!

RICH: I bet you jumped.

BEEFY: I was in the air.

RICH: He thought he was a goner.

BEEFY: He turned him upside down.

RICH: By the ankles.

BEEFY: Shook him like a rat.

          (*They take their time over the memory of the moment.*)

BEEFY: Did you finish reading it to me?

RICH: Not the second time.

         (*BEEFY thumbs through the book.*)

RICH: You should take it with you.

BEEFY: Very funny.

RICH: You could try.

BEEFY: Don't be dull.

RICH: Well, take it anyway.

BEEFY: There's no point. (*He throws the book down.*)

RICH: Beefy?

BEEFY: What?

RICH: When you're in the bookies, how do you know what horses are running?

BEEFY: Well, I look at the wall, don't I? What do you think I do, phone the jockeys and ask 'em personally?

RICH: Yes, but how do you know what they are, how do you read them?

BEEFY: I don't. I learn 'em. I look at the shapes of the words and I learn 'em.

RICH: But Beefy, that's reading.

BEEFY: No it's not, it's remembering shapes.

RICH: Yeah, it's called reading.

BEEFY: Look, horses I can read, words I can't.

RICH: Bet you could read that. (*holds the book out to him*)

BEEFY: Only if Shergar turns up in the last chapter, and I don't think he does. Forget it Rich, I'm a natural dunce.

RICH: Well, take it anyway. You might find someone to

read it for you.

BEEFY: Listen —

RICH: Look. (*Silence.*)

BEEFY: Suppose I could always use it as an offensive weapon.

(*He takes the book.*)

RICH: Well, there you are: a whistle, a poker and *Great Expectations*. What more does a man need?

BEEFY: Nothing.

RICH: So, you're all set for the road.

BEEFY: Aye, on the road again.

RICH: The road to Mandalay.

BEEFY: Road to nowhere.

RICH: Off the road to Morocco.

BEEFY: Thunder road.

RICH: The road to Singapore.

BEEFY: Lonesome road.

RICH: Yellow Brick road.

BEEFY: Abbey Road.

RICH: Road to Utopia.

BEEFY: Road to freedom.

(*They are both looking out of the window.*)

RICH: Where are you going?

BEEFY: I don't know.

RICH: Just keep to the road.

BEEFY: And don't look back.

RICH: But don't cheat.

BEEFY:	And don't lie.
RICH:	I don't.
BEEFY:	Nor me.
	(*They stare at one another.*)
RICH:	You'd better have the letter then.
BEEFY:	What letter?
RICH:	The letter that didn't come this morning.
	(*He gets out the letter. BEEFY stares at it in disbelief.*)
BEEFY:	You had it all the time.
RICH:	Yes.
BEEFY:	Why didn't you give it to me when I asked? (*nothing*) Say, why the hell didn't you just give it to me?
RICH:	I forgot.
BEEFY:	No, you didn't.
RICH:	No, I lied.
BEEFY:	You lied. You stand there and admit to me that you lied. Just like that. Why mun, why?
RICH:	I don't know.
BEEFY:	No, you never know, do you? You just do it. All the time you just do it for the sake of it. Give it here. (*He looks at the address on the envelope.*) See, it's Splott, it's not Splow at all, it's Splott. What does that say on the top by there.
RICH:	Beefy.
BEEFY:	Well that's me, innit? Not you, it's me.
RICH:	Yes.
	(*Absolute silence.*)
BEEFY:	So? What does it say then? What does this letter

addressed to me actually say?

RICH: Read it.

(*BEEFY gets it out and looks at it.*)

BEEFY: I can't.

RICH: You can read the horses, you can read that.

BEEFY: If there were horses in there I would, but there's not a single horse in that letter, so I can't. You read it out to me. (*thrusts him the letter*)

RICH: It says the council will soon be making improvements... to tidy up the place... for the benefit of residents.

BEEFY: What residents? We're the only ones here. It can't just say that. You're making it up. Read it properly like a real letter, "dear sir" and all that.

RICH: Dear Sir. Or Madam. In our efforts to serve the community and improve the environment we intend to tidy up the place for the benefit of residents. Yours faithfully, someone I can't read, on the council. That's the letter, that's what it says.

BEEFY: Rubbish.

RICH: It's there, black and white from the council.

BEEFY: I don't believe it. No one does anything for us.

RICH: Well, they are now. Serving the community. And that's me.

BEEFY: Let me have a butchers at that.

(*BEEFY takes the letter. RICH surveys the scene outside the window.*)

RICH: Yes, I can picture it now.

BEEFY: I flaming well can't.

RICH: A row of gaily painted charabancs. Individual gardens, roses climbing up the trellis, hanging baskets. They'll probably have a shower block: rivers and waterfalls of constant hot water, perfect, tiny tablets of scented soap, free and on demand.

BEEFY: What's this, insp... inspect... Seven o'clock inspection, they've had a seven o'clock inspection. (*back to letter*) Seven day... Seven Day Wonder, he was running at Plumpton last week, I'm sure, fell at the first. Demol... demolition, Demolition Dancer, that's that grey mare beaten by a neck years ago in the National. Qui... quit, Mr. Quitter, pig of an horse he was, cost me a fortune. Removal, Removal Man, now there was an 'orse, won real money on him. (*adds up the letter*)

BEEFY: Seven o'clock inspection. Seven Day Wonder, Demolition Dancer, Mister Quitter, Removal Man.

RICH: Could be an idyll here, a haven, paradise.

BEEFY: You been lying again.

RICH: Just picturing how it could be, painting the world through our window.

BEEFY: Seven o'clock inspection, Seven Day Wonder, Demolition Dancer, Mister Quitter, Removal Man. Mean anything to you?

RICH: Runners in the two-thirty at Haydock?

BEEFY: You know damn well what it is. They are going to demolish this place, and you have got seven days to quit or they will remove you. That's right, isn't it? Isn't it?

RICH: Something like that.

BEEFY: Well, why the hell didn't you tell me?

RICH: You'd make a fuss.

BEEFY: No, I wouldn't. I'd just go. And you'd have to as well. No fuss, just shift.

RICH: Not me.

BEEFY: What?

RICH: I'm not going.

BEEFY: Rich, they will chuck you off this dump like sand off a shovel.

RICH: See, you're making a fuss. That's why I lied.

BEEFY: I'm not fussing.

RICH: Well, leave me alone then. I'll stay, you go. Simple as that.

BEEFY: Why the hell do you want to stay? It's a dump.

RICH: It's home.

BEEFY: It's a clapped-out caravan.

RICH: It's got character.

BEEFY: Oh yeah, it's got character. No roof and half a floor but it's got character.

RICH: It's got potential.

BEEFY: Where, for god's sake?

RICH: Out there.

           (*He gazes out of the window. BEEFY takes a good look as well.*)

BEEFY: Rich, tell me, what exactly do you see out there?

RICH: The view.

BEEFY: Yeah?

RICH: Well, I can see the houses, chimneys and smudges of smoke, the river, the road, the place where the road meets the trees, where the trees meet the sand, where the sand meets the sky. Window on the world.

BEEFY: Rich, there is no sand out there, it's mud. Mud as

40

far as the eye can see. Flat mud, mud flats. No little chimneys and smudges of smoke, just burning bits of houses. It's a bomb site, a shithole, an open toilet as far as the eye can see.

RICH: No, no, you're not seeing it right.

BEEFY: I'm seeing it dead on.

RICH: You don't know how to look and dream.

BEEFY: That's not dreams out there, that's lies.

RICH: What do you know about it?

BEEFY: I know the difference.

RICH: You know the difference between a horse and a greyhound and that's it. And you don't dream you just cheat and that is all.

BEEFY: You think so, do you?

RICH: Yes, I do.

BEEFY: Right.

RICH: Right.

BEEFY: Right.

          (*'Jumping Jack Flash' by the Rolling Stones, turned all the way up, begins to play.*)

BEEFY: Right, dreamer, liar, dance in the fire. Cop a load of this window on the world.

          (*BEEFY puts on headband and shades. He pushes RICH in the wheelchair.*)

RICH: What are you doing?

BEEFY: Live fast, die young.

RICH: I'm too old to die young.

BEEFY: Not in your dreams, Richie.

          (*BEEFY gets behind RICH'S back and traps him in the*

wheelchair with his stick. BEEFY uses the stick as a motorbike handlebars and snarls the lyrics into RICH'S ear.)

BEEFY: You with me, Rich?

RICH: No.

BEEFY: You ready for more.

RICH: No.

BEEFY: Good, let's burn rubber and torch the tarmac.

(BEEFY ties his headband round RICH'S eyes, and then pulls RICH'S hat right down over his face completely, blinding him. He then sets the chair in a spin and pushes him off. BEEFY then sits down and watches RICH as the music trails away.)

BEEFY: How's that for a dream?

RICH: It was a nightmare.

BEEFY: No, it was a lie. I haven't got a motorbike. And I've never ridden a motorbike, and I'm never going to either, am I? *(Silence.)*

RICH: Well...

BEEFY: I am never going to ride a motorbike, never ever, not while there's a hole in your arse. It's not going to happen. Can you see that?

RICH: Well...

BEEFY: Look at me. I am never going to ride a motorbike, am I?

RICH: Possibly not.

BEEFY: Definitely not. And why not? Because I'm a short, fat bastard?

RICH: No.

BEEFY: No Rich, you're right. Not because I'm a short fat bastard. Because I'm a short, fat, bastard cripple.

RICH: No.

BEEFY: Yes. Say it, Rich. I'm a short, fat, bastard cripple.

RICH: No, no, it's not true.

BEEFY: Yes, yes, too right it's fucking true. Me on a motorbike is a dream. But I know it is. Just like I know that out there is a lie. It's not paradise, it's not a haven, it's a dump. And the only thing it's ever going to be is a bigger dump.

RICH: Well, it could be...

BEEFY: Look at it, for god's sake. What do you see? And don't lie.

(RICH looks for a long time.)

RICH: It's a dump.

BEEFY: It's a dump.

RICH: But it's a dream, Beefy.

BEEFY: No. Dreams are the business. And you don't have any business, do you?

RICH: I do.

BEEFY: Like what? Like this junk in here. *(BEEFY starts to hurl things out of the trolley.)* Painter, gardener, security guard, sky flaming pilot. You weren't any of these, were you? *(silence)* Were you, Rich?

RICH: No.

BEEFY: No, all lies. No dreams, no business, just lies.

(RICH surveys the debris, picks up the paint brush.)

RICH: Could have been a painter.

BEEFY: Aye, and I could have been a jockey.

RICH: Yeah?

BEEFY: Yeah.

RICH:	Could you?
BEEFY:	What?
RICH:	Could you have been a jockey?
BEEFY:	No. Not in a million years. I lied. Wanted it so much I lied. My father worked in a knackers' yard. He cut up horses. He didn't ride 'em, he cut 'em up. And I didn't ride 'em either. Never. Never ever.

(Silence.)

RICH:	Not a dream between us then.
BEEFY:	No.
RICH:	Not a bean.
BEEFY:	Nothing.
RICH:	No dreams, no business, nothing.

(They take their time to consider this, themselves, the audience, each other.)

BEEFY: I'd like an horse. Big fat mare, wide as a barge and built like a tank. I could watch it ambling round the field sniffing for clover. Or it could pull things: rocks, barges, stupid cars stuck in the mud. Or I'd ride it, up on its back, short in the saddle and safe as an armchair. Coasting the lanes, slow and easy like an idling Norton Commando. Looking down on the world. Me on an 'orse, riding the world. *(Silence.)* Need a jackpot on the geegees first though, don't I?

(He starts putting things back in the trolley.)

RICH:	She could pull this.
BEEFY:	Who could pull what?
RICH:	Your horse. She could pull this caravan.
BEEFY:	Rich, one tug from me and this place would fall to

bits.

RICH: Yes. So I'll do it up. Paint it, repair it, turn it into a real home. You go off on the road, find your horse, come back and it can pull the wagon. It'll be a proper mobile home.

BEEFY: You won't be here. They'll have shifted you. These people mean business.

RICH: So do I. And dreams are the business.

BEEFY: Rich!

RICH: I'll make it happen. It's a dream, but I'll make it happen. Now you go and make yours happen. Get your horse.

BEEFY: I won't get an 'orse.

RICH: So its a lie.

BEEFY: No.

RICH: So go and get one. How much are they?

BEEFY: I don't know, a couple of hundred.

(*RICH picks up the answering machine and drops it into BEEFY'S bag.*)

RICH: There, should get a few quid for that. Start you off, buy you a front forelock or something.

BEEFY: Horses don't have forelocks.

RICH: Oh.

BEEFY: They have fetlocks.

(*RICH opens some paint pots.*)

BEEFY: You can't paint. You can't even knock in a nail.

RICH: And you can't ride a horse.

BEEFY: I'd look good on a horse. I've got the walk of a cowboy. I've been told that before. (*Silence.*) Have to find some decent grass for her. Not a single

45

	blade out there.
RICH:	Just as well they're shifting us.
BEEFY:	I know what horses like. Not much about horses I don't know.
RICH:	You've followed them.
BEEFY:	I have.

(*He looks out of the window.*)

BEEFY:	I could still go off...
RICH:	Of course.
BEEFY:	By myself.
RICH:	Certainly.
BEEFY:	With the horse.
RICH:	Idling the lanes like a Norton Commando. Eh, you could call it Norton.
BEEFY:	Commando's better.
RICH:	Yamaha.
BEEFY:	Kawasaki.
RICH:	Triumph.
BEEFY:	Bonneville.
RICH:	Harley.
BEEFY:	Davison.
RICH:	Bantam.
BEEFY:	I think Commando's best.
RICH:	And we'll call the charabanc Norton.
BEEFY:	Rich, it's not a charabanc.
RICH:	It's a caravan.
BEEFY:	It's a caravan.

RICH: Think I'll start with a sign, bit of a protest, "Hands Off Norton".

BEEFY: Aye. Think I'll start with Cheltenham. Gold Cup. Always been lucky for me, Cheltenham.

RICH: You were arrested in Cheltenham.

BEEFY: Was not.

RICH: Were.

BEEFY: Was not. (*stops*) I was. Twice. Not many places I haven't been arrested.

RICH: No.

(RICH hands BEEFY the crash helmet with great ceremony. BEEFY tosses it in the trolley, takes his stick and makes his way out.)

BEEFY: Never been arrested for dancing, though.

RICH: I have.

(BEEFY leaves. RICH stops painting, searches through the records, puts one on, goes back to his painting. We hear 'On The Road Again' by Canned Heat.)

End

The Best Years of Our Lives

The Best Years of Our Lives was first performed by the Made in Wales Stage Company on 7th March, 1990 at Emlyn Williams Theatre, Theatre Clwyd, Mold with the following cast:

EDDIE	Boyd Clack
SAL	Lynne Hunter
NEIL	Brian Hibbard
GLEN	Nina Holloway
CLEM	Roger Watkins
ROB	Nicholas Pritchard
FIONA	Helen Gwyn
TERRY	Rhodri Hugh
VOICE OVER	Dominic Hingorani

Production Team

DIRECTOR	Jamie Garven
DESIGNER	Kim Kenny
LIGHTING	Keith Hemming
STAGE MANAGEMENT	Peter Grundy
	Russell Harvey
	Karen Jennings
	Phillippa Malbon

Author's Note

The play was written in 1989 and set in the near future of 1995. It predicted that the last nationalised colliery would be closed that year and by then a Labour government would be in power, albeit one that was indistinguishable from its predecessor. I was one and two years out respectively in my first two predictions. I am still waiting for history to disprove the third. The play can be performed retaining these dates and be seen more or less historically accurate or the 'FINAL SHIFT' scene can be jettisoned, and it can then be set at any time with the adjustment of any inappropriate dates.

Act One

Final Shift

(*Lights of a Juke Box. 'Blue Bayou' by Roy Orbison is playing. Lights and music fade to cinema blackness. A large screen is lit up with the face of Rob Bentley. He is talking to unseen questioners.*)

ROB: Regeneration. Regeneration and rebirth. Those are the words I would prefer to use. (*pause*) No. No, no, no. That is a word we have removed from our vocabulary. May traitors flinch and cowards... no, certainly not. Homage yes, but betrayal never. A homage to our heritage. (*pause*) I really think we should start using the same language. This is not a wake, it's a celebration. Of our history, our heritage. And if we can agree on one common word may I suggest that it be rejoice. Yes, rejoice. Rejoice, rejoice, rejoice.

(*There is a long blast of a hooter. The picture freezes and an ambiguous political emblem [A rose on a union jack] and the date, 1994, is superimposed on the screen. The picture goes. In the darkness three men in blackened orange overalls are fleetingly seen in a barrage of flash cameras. Strong television lights are suddenly turned on them.*)

EDDIE: How do you think we feel?

NEIL: Over the cowing moon.

EDDIE: Delirious?

NEIL: Chuffed to bastard bits?

51

CLEM: Well, we're not.

EDDIE: No.

NEIL: No.

EDDIE: We're sick.

NEIL: As bleeding pigs.

CLEM: A good part of our lives down there. End now, innit? Seal it up, kiss her goodbye.

NEIL: Aye, kiss her sodding —

CLEM: Bitter? No, not bitter.

NEIL: Just twisted.

EDDIE: Listen, how would you feel, eh? If they closed you down. Shut you up. The last channel, the final rag. No, I know, they wouldn't, would they? We'll always need you. To dig over the dirt.

CLEM: Yes, we do know what progress means.

EDDIE: It means talking to you buggers.

NEIL: And I'll spell it out for you. (*spits*) Don't look back.

(*The television lights go out. They all look back.*)

NEIL: 'Cos there's sod all there. (*They turn back. Cans are cracked open. They start to strip off.*) Choke on that, suckers. (*takes a swig*) King coal is dead.

EDDIE: Long live redundancy.

NEIL: All fifty grand of it.

CLEM: To piss against the wall.

NEIL: Me? Joke, is it? This is an 'ead on my shoulders not a bastard beach ball. Property, that's where my smackers are going. A big bastard house on a big bastard hill where I can watch all the poor little bastards down below.

(*CLEM and EDDIE look at one another.*)

EDDIE: Bastard astronaut.

NEIL: My feet are on the ground, Eddie boy. You won't see me stuck on my fat arse.

EDDIE: Well that's where I'll be. Age of leisure, innit Clem?

NEIL: Listen to him. Electric Eddie the man with the clockwork cooker. You haven't got a sodding clue, have you?

EDDIE: Nor a big bastard house.

NEIL: I am not just talking houses. I am talking world view here, new life. I am talking new job.

EDDIE: You can't have a job, you're redundant.

NEIL: Clem. Tell him.

CLEM: He's selling his body.

NEIL: Body be buggered. I am going into security.

EDDIE: What? Protection, you mean?

NEIL: Security, security: alarms, locks, trip switches. I'm selling 'em. (*They look at him blankly.*) Look, every rich plonker who moves up here is scared shitless of the poor plonkers who live next door. So what do they want? Security. In a big way. It's a growth industry. I'll clean up.

EDDIE: So you're going on the knocker then, are you?

CLEM: Mister Bettaware.

EDDIE: You'll need a big case for all them locks.

NEIL: Bleeding dark ages, you pair. I am talking the Hitachi Security System. That means the Hitachi company car, the Hitachi cellular phone, the Hitachi complete caboodle. Bastard case. Digital filofax, that's me boy.

EDDIE: Right.

CLEM: With you.

NEIL: You'll wish you were. I'm not going to sit and
           stink.

EDDIE: Nor me. Like I said, it's leisure, innit? That's what
           I'll be working on.

CLEM: Eddie, you don't work at leisure. It's the opposite,
           mun.

EDDIE: I know exactly what it is and I'll be clocking on at
           the leisure centre first thing Monday morning.

CLEM: Aye. Why not.

NEIL: And what about you Clem, swanning off to some
           costa?

CLEM: I got plans. Like you said, new life now.

NEIL: Yeah, right. Goodbye black stuff. Hello green
           grass. (*Drinks, goes off whistling 'Green Grass'. The
           other two follow. Cinema blackness. Footage of the pit
           closing now appears on the screen. This includes the
           initial interview with the men. There is a Pathe News
           type voice over.*)

NEWSREEL: A momentous day in Wales this week. For almost
           two hundred years the gallant men of the South
           Wales coalfield have brought fuel to the nation
           from the bowels of the earth. But this week the
           curtain came down on the final act of one of
           industry's most turbulent dramas as the last shift
           ended in the last pit in Wales. For some it is the
           timely ending of an era, for others a new
           beginning. But for the colliery itself it is a new
           lease of life as it will form the centrepiece of the
           Industrial Heritage Trail which will bring wealth
           and work flooding back into these proud valleys
           once again. Meanwhile in Northern Ireland
           another British regiment prepares to leave the
           province. New challenges await these boys too,
           and for some, the quieter frontiers of civilian life.

(A squaddie turns toward the camera, the picture freezes. Blackout.)

Housewarming

(A hand held torch is immediately switched on. As the light grows a figure is faintly seen. We see that the man is in his twenties wearing what appears to be the remains of a soldier's uniform: t-shirt, khaki trousers. He shines the torch around the room. There is no furniture but on the floor there is a cordless phone, a bottle of wine and a bunch of red roses.)

TERRY: Welcome home. Our boys. Your boys. Home from the front. Creeping in through the back door of your brains. Back from all the sticky little corners, all the black, grubby holes. Leaving neat, little prints of shite all over your bright new carpet. *(picks up the phone, speaks into it)* Hi, I'm not here right now but if you'd like to leave a message, just start talking. *(pause)* Hello, is there anybody there? You don't know me, but I know you. *(puts the phone down)* Brave old boys. All home to roost. *(clicks off the torch and leaves)*

(cut to)

(The lights come on full, revealing the same scene. Phone, wine and roses. Glen walks in, looks around as if for the first time. NEIL'S voice is heard off.)

NEIL: Glen! Glen! *(appears)* What the hell is this?

GLEN: Looks like —

NEIL: I know what it is. Shit. All over the floor.

GLEN: Funny.

NEIL: Well, where's it from?

GLEN: Don't look at me. They're boots. Men's boots.

NEIL: Men?

GLEN: Thought we were going to be on an 'ill. Big house on a hill. It's not big, it's a shoebox. Clean white cardboard.

NEIL: It is not bloody clean. Someone has walked shit right through the damn place.

GLEN: Perhaps we're in the wrong house.

NEIL: What?

GLEN: Wrong house. They all looked the same. Perhaps it doesn't matter where you go. Musical houses. You don't notice till you find yourself in bed with some strange —

NEIL: Shut up, you silly cow. This is our house and some dirty booted bugger has got in first and left.... (*He spots the wine and roses.*)

GLEN: Some wine and roses.

NEIL: What are those for?

GLEN: To hide the smell of the —

NEIL: Shut up. Shit, wine and roses, what's going on?

GLEN: Funny people. Funny people live up here, Neil. Not us.

NEIL: There's nothing funny about shit, wine and bloody — (*He grabs the roses, sees a card, stops and reads.*) Funny people, eh? Well read that then. Go on. That'll make you smile.

GLEN: (*reading*) "Fraternal greetings to newcomers Neil and Glen, from your new neighbours Rob and Fiona. Welcome to Hetty Park."

NEIL.   Welcome. Fraternal. What do you think of that then?

GLEN: How do they know our names?

NEIL: They took the trouble to find out. Obviously. That's the sort of people who live here. Our sort.

GLEN: We don't drink wine.

NEIL: Look Glen, people do things differently here. They drink wine, make phone calls, wear suits —

GLEN: Walk about with shit on their shoes.

NEIL: That could happen to anyone. Come on Glen, this is the first day in our new house. New life, remember? Now stop twitching and enjoy it. (*She stares at him blankly.*) En-joy it.

GLEN: How did they get in?

NEIL: Jesu Christ, through the bastard cat flap, I don't know.

            (*Voices are heard off.*)

VOICE: Hello. Anybody home?

NEIL: Who's that?

GLEN: I don't know, but you'd better get a mat for their feet.

NEIL: Shut up. (*Calls out.*) Hello. We're in here.

            (*Enter ROB and FIONA BENTLEY.*)

ROB: Hello there. We saw the van. I'm Rob Bentley, my wife, Fiona. We live at the top of the drive.

NEIL: Oh, you're — (*points to the bottle*)

FIONA: Yes, I hope you don't mind.

ROB: But we thought, you know, empty house —

FIONA: Nothing like Rioja to warm it up.

NEIL: No. Nothing.

ROB: Just thought we'd show our noses and break the ice.

NEIL: Aye. Course.

GLEN: How did you get in?

FIONA: Oh, sorry. We saw the agent, he let us in. Hope you don't mind.

NEIL: No. No problem. She was just wondering like. (*pause*) We've just moved in.

FIONA: Yes, we saw the van. (*pause*)

NEIL: Look, why don't I open this now?

FIONA: No, no, that's for you.

NEIL: No, we may as well, mun. Where's the corkscrew, Glen?

GLEN: We haven't got a corkscrew.

NEIL: We have.

GLEN: We haven't

NEIL: We have.

GLEN: There might be one on your scout knife.

FIONA: There's no need really.

NEIL: No, like you said, break the ice. (*He starts to tear at the wrapping.*)

ROB: It's a good estate this. Tidy houses too.

GLEN: Shoeboxes. Have I seen you somewhere before?

ROB: Um, could have I suppose.

FIONA: It's a small world.

GLEN: What do you do?

ROB: Er, a bit at the Poly.

GLEN: No.

ROB: Bit at the Cultural Centre.

GLEN: No.

ROB: Even less at the Council.

GLEN: No.

FIONA: Perhaps you once shared a seat on a bus.

(*NEIL is now trying to thrust the cork into the bottle with his thumb.*)

ROB: Look Neil, I'm sure I've got something back at the house.

NEIL: No problem. This'll do the trick.

GLEN: You're Councillor Bentley. I've seen you at the Institute, haven't I?

ROB: I was at a meeting there, yes. Oh, you're one of the women who work there.

GLEN: In the cinema.

NEIL: Fleapit.

GLEN: I help to run it.

NEIL: Usherette.

GLEN: What were you doing there?

ROB: Well, it's a bit confidential at the moment.

FIONA: That means it's the Heritage Trail.

ROB: Fiona.

NEIL: (*now almost prising off the bottleneck with his bare hands*) Bloody miners' museums. Mad, mun. Paid us thousands to bring us up, now they're going to charge a packet to get people back down there. No sense.

GLEN: Neil was a miner.

FIONA: Rob is chair of the Heritage Committee.

(*NEIL freezes with the bottle.*)

NEIL: Look — don't get me wrong — I'm not saying I'm against it — no.

ROB: No, I take your point. But I don't think we can turn our backs on our heritage. It's all important.

Colliery, chapel —

NEIL:	Bookies. (*Nobody laughs.*) Joke.
FIONA:	Don't tempt him.
ROB:	So what do you do now anyway, Neil?
GLEN:	He's starting a new —
NEIL:	I can tell 'em... I got a new job... security... selling it... alarms and stuff... I'll have a look at your gaff if you like, you need it round here... Jesus Christ, why don't they put this stuff in cans?
FIONA:	It doesn't matter really.
NEIL:	No, I'll have it off now.
ROB:	We could always go to the wine bar.
NEIL:	Bog off, we don't need no poncey wine bar.
FIONA:	I wouldn't call it poncey.
NEIL:	Why not?
ROB:	Probably because she runs it.

(*NEIL is transfixed.*)

GLEN:	We've never been in. Wine's not really our cup of tea.
NEIL:	Right. Corkscrew, toolbox. One minute.

(*He goes out. Silence.*)

GLEN:	Do many people use it? The wine bar.
FIONA:	It's getting better.
ROB:	Double figures now.
FIONA:	It'll pick up.
ROB:	When?
FIONA:	Perhaps when your Heritage Trail gets off the ground.

ROB: It's not my Heritage Trail. It's the community's.

GLEN: Perhaps because it's foreign. It's the same in the cinema.

ROB: You serve wine in the cinema?

GLEN: No, films. Foreign films. We're making our own.

ROB: Wine?

GLEN: No, film. We've made one before. About the strike. This is a sort of follow up. Ten years on.

FIONA: Not just an usherette then.

ROB: And it's not just a fleapit, believe you me.

GLEN: You'll come and see it then.

ROB: Well, if we get a chance.

            (*NEIL returns brandishing a large screwdriver.*)

NEIL: Right. Vino beano, here we go.

FIONA: Glen's just been telling us about her film.

NEIL: That film's over. New picture now. Isn't that right, Rob?

ROB: Well, things have moved on.

NEIL: Aye and left sodding films behind.

FIONA: Well, I'd like to see it. Perhaps I can have a preview when you're next in work.

NEIL: No chance. She's not going.

GLEN: Not this week, no.

NEIL: Not this week, next week, never.

GLEN: Who says?

NEIL: No one says. It just is.

GLEN: Neil, it's my job.

NEIL: Was. Like I said, new picture now and that part's

	gone. Cut.
ROB:	Look, perhaps we should call back.
NEIL:	No. We're having a bevvy, right?
ROB:	Well —
NEIL:	No well, we're drinking this wine. Aren't we, Fiona?
FIONA:	If you insist, Neil.
NEIL:	I do. And I'm insisting here. Right, Glen?
GLEN:	It's my job.
NEIL:	It's not a job, it's a bloody joke. Do you know what she does? She sells ice cream. Trolls about with a box of lollies hanging from her neck. Would you let Fiona do that? No, course you bloody wouldn't. And you wouldn't want to anyway, would you?
GLEN:	She sells wine.
NEIL:	What?
FIONA:	The wine bar.
NEIL:	Well, that's another story, innit? There's a bloody big difference between serving wine and doling out choc ices.
GLEN:	Yes. It's a lot slower.
NEIL:	Oh yes, here we go. See, that's the sort of lip she picks up working in that hole. With those smartarse women. Well, it's gone now. Dead and gone. Bastard buried. Especially that fucking job!
	(*The word explodes the atmosphere. When the dust settles, the phone rings. They all look at it.*)
FIONA:	It's all happening, isn't it?
NEIL:	Answer it then.

GLEN: No-one knows our number.

NEIL: Some bugger does.

GLEN: I don't know our number.

NEIL: Answer it.

         (*She does nothing.*)

FIONA: Shall I –

NEIL: No. It's her house, her phone. Now pick it up.

         (*She moves to the phone and picks it up.*)

GLEN: Hello... hello...

NEIL: Who is it?

GLEN: Hello... this is... (*reading*) four, o, one, three, three, nine. Hello.

NEIL: Who is it? Ask them who's speaking.

GLEN: No-one. No-one speaking.

NEIL: Well ask them!

GLEN: Nothing. No pips. Nobody. Someone –

FIONA: I should hang up if I were you.

GLEN: Someone playing –

NEIL: Jesus Christ.

GLEN: Playing tricks.

NEIL: Tell 'em then!

FIONA: Just put it down.

GLEN: Who is it?

NEIL: For god's sake. (*marches over, grabs phone*) Piss off, moron! (*slams it down*) There.

FIONA: Funny people.

ROB: Cranks.

GLEN: I don't like it.

NEIL: Shut up.

GLEN: Don't like this house.

NEIL: Shut up.

GLEN: We shouldn't have moved up here.

NEIL: Will you shut your stupid, twitchy... this is our house. We're living here and we're having a glass of wine. (*He starts pushing at the screwdriver with renewed vigour.*) This... is where... we... belong! (*The cork is plunged into the bottle and the wine splurges everywhere. NEIL looks around with manic triumph.*)

Exile

(*Light of a reading lamp. CLEM is hunched over a small table. On it are an exercise book and a packet of Oxo cubes. He is holding a pen. In front of him are some large, impressive looking tomes.*)

CLEM: (*He picks up one of the books.*) Why is history so bloody heavy? I'll kick the bucket before I make the weight. (*drops the book, takes up his pencil*) Pencil and paper. I'm like a bloody big kid. (*looks at the pencil in his hand*) Hold it like a chisel. Be better off. Chip it all out and shovel it on then. Fill up the pages like trucks. (*He pauses, then starts to write.*) Forty years underground. Nineteen fifty-four. Eddie Cochran, Carl Perkins, Roy... no, they were later. Nineteen fifty-four. Elvis, mun, 'That's alright Mama'. Forty years of rock and roll, forty years of.... Bloody hell. (*throws down the pen*) Losing the scent. Musn't. Got to get it right. (*He picks up a book, searches through it as if for some inspiration.*) No. (*He puts the books down, unwraps an Oxo cube, crumbles it, then sniffs his fingers.*) Turn your bloody guts. Every day — first day. Broken thermos in my duffle bag. Brown bitty goo in my sandwiches. Through the gates. This colliery is now managed by the National Coal Board. On behalf of the people. Slogans. Dai Francis at Porthcawl, the Arabs won't live in tents forever. Too right, we're the ones in bloody wigwams now. Porthcawl on a Saturday night. (*There is a noise off.*) Who's that? Anyone there? (*silence*) Ghosts. (*shouts out*) I don't need no bloody ghosts. (*picks up the book, enviously*) Just want the real thing here. Porthcawl. Saturday night. Roy Orbison. Shit! Forty years of junk and jingles. It can't boil down to that. There was more. Much more.

(*cut to*)

(*Enormous sound of Roy Orbison's 'Only the Lonely'. We see EDDIE, headphones on, guitar on this lap, can of lager at his lips, empties at his feet. He is singing along to the record. SAL comes in and turns off the music with a remote control.*)

SAL: Eddie. You are a mess.

EDDIE: I'm going to reform.

SAL: Good. Start with this, shall we? (*takes can from him*)

EDDIE: The band. Reform the band. Eddie and the Electricians. What do you think?

SAL: They're all dead, deaf or fat. I have got some news.

(*EDDIE takes off the headset.*)

SAL: Eddie, I'd like to talk. That's part of leisure, isn't it?

EDDIE: Yep.

SAL: Well?

EDDIE: You want to talk about work.

SAL: Eddie! Will you listen. Please!

EDDIE: Shoot. (*He starts to play.*)

SAL: Right. News. The film. The one I've been making for three thousand years. They're finally going to show it, at the Institute. We've fixed the date. Ten years to the day. Since the strike. Big do, proper show. But I'll need your help before. With the film. You and Clem. What do you think?

EDDIE: Sounds like work. Your work.

SAL: Ours.

EDDIE: What do you think of my idea?

SAL: Eddie, you're dreaming. (*She makes to go.*)

EDDIE: I've changed the plugs. Checked the wiring. Best to really.

SAL: Eddie.

EDDIE: Have a look, check 'em out. You won't fault it.

SAL: Eddie, you are just... (*She gives up and goes out.*)

EDDIE: Useless. Like a rusty screwdriver.

    (*He cracks open another can, puts the headset back on. SAL comes back in.*)

SAL: Eddie, what have you done with the food? (*She takes off the headset.*) The food? Where's it gone?

EDDIE: What do I want with food?

SAL: I don't know but it's gone. Tins of it. What the hell are you playing at?

EDDIE: Don't need food to play.

SAL: Eddie! Do something. You can't just play.

EDDIE: Why not? It's leisure innit?

SAL: No! It's not bloody leisure. It's nothing.

EDDIE: Oh no, better than nothing. It's next to nothing.

SAL: Look, about the band. You could play at the do. After the film. Like the benefits. What do you think?

EDDIE: Try it out. (*puts the headset back on*)

SAL: You've got to help me out with the film first though. You and Clem. Next week. OK? (*He says nothing.*) OK. (*She goes.*)

EDDIE: Tins of food. Don't work, don't eat. Simple. (*drinks*)

(*cut to*)

(*Lights pick out TERRY. He is crouching, eating salmon out of a tin with the blade of a knife.*)

TERRY: An army marches on its stomach. And watches and waits. I see you. Pinko infantry storming the wine bars. Capturing the high ground. The hi-fis. Sitting there fat and shiny, clogged with quiche. Lording it, larding it. Wiping a greasy smile off your chops. Soft life's hard, innit? For the hard men. Soft boys. Smug bastards. (*He drops the can and disappears.*)

Homecoming

(*The Institute. EDDIE is arranging equipment on stage: amp, mike, guitar. He looks up to the box as if to check the correct position. When he appears satisfied, he leaves. ROB and NEIL walk in from the back of the auditorium. They are followed by GLEN. She is looking distraught and dishevelled.*)

ROB: If I were you.

GLEN: Neil.

NEIL: If you was me.

ROB: If I were you.

NEIL: If you was me.

GLEN: Neil.

ROB: Such a waste.

NEIL: I bloody know.

GLEN: Neil.

NEIL: What!

GLEN: I need to talk.

NEIL: Time and place, Glen. This is business. Now wrap up.

ROB: Could bring in thousands. And I'm not talking fleas. Upgrading, highlighting, change the profile.

NEIL: Not this dump, me.

ROB: Same goes. Upgrading, highlighting, change the profile.

NEIL: Serious, mun.

ROB: I am serious. So you want to be serious?

NEIL: Aye , serious.

ROB: Honest?

NEIL: Honest.

ROB: Brutal?

NEIL: Brutal.

ROB: No holds barred?

NEIL: On the bastard chin.

ROB: Shall we start?

NEIL: When you're ready.

ROB: You're a lout.

NEIL:	What?
ROB:	Is that how you talk to your customers? On the bastard —
NEIL:	No.
ROB:	How then?
NEIL:	Proper like.
ROB:	Like a proper lout.
NEIL:	Now listen, pal.
ROB:	Brutal and honest. OK? (*NEIL backs off.*) You're selling security and talking like a thug.
NEIL:	If people don't like the way I talk —
ROB:	Exactly, the way. Accent yes, fine. Equals accessibility. But moderate it. If your language stinks so might your product.
NEIL:	Brutal you said, not bloody vicious.
ROB:	Just warming up. The jewellery, lose it.
GLEN:	He's always had that.
ROB:	Glen, would you buy a burglar alarm from a Gypsy? Roots are all very well but don't wear them in your ear. (*He starts to take the earring out. ROB flicks his jacket.*)
ROB:	That can go as well.
NEIL:	It's brand new.
GLEN:	I bought it for him.
ROB:	Well now get one that fits. You look like a spiv. Security from the back of a lorry? No-one wants that.
NEIL:	Anything else?
ROB:	Yes, your hair.

NEIL: I've just had it cut.

ROB: No. You've had it shortened. Like a hem. Neil, you're in a hi-tech world looking like a potato farmer. It won't wash.

NEIL: No, it bloody won't. I get the picture alright. I'm a spivvy lout. Well if that's what I am then that's what I am.

ROB: Change.

NEIL: I can't change.

ROB: The packaging. We all have to sometimes if the product's not shifting. Selling's like politics. It's a front. Just needs the right dressing. Three A's. Authority, accessibility and... adaptability. Otherwise —

NEIL: You wind up selling spuds.

ROB: Or digging them. Change the profile. The only way. (*He looks around.*) Look, no hard feelings, OK? Let's just slot that chat in the business hole.

NEIL: Aye, business.

GLEN: Frankenstein's monster.

NEIL: Who?

GLEN: You. Me.

NEIL: Look, what the hell are you doing here anyway? You should be at tai-chi.

ROB: With Fiona.

NEIL: And at the wine bar in five minutes. What you bloody playing at?

GLEN: I think I'm turning Japanese.

NEIL: What?

GLEN: I told 'em. I think I'm turning Japanese. And left. I wanted to tell you. To talk.

NEIL: Time and bloody place, Glen. Later, alright.

           (*EDDIE is suddenly spotlit at the back of the stage. He has a guitar and launches into 'In Dreams'.*)

NEIL: Jesus Christ. Oi. Oi. Oi. (*EDDIE stops the guitar.*) We're in here.

EDDIE: No. I'm in here.

NEIL: This is business, right.

EDDIE: And this is rehearsing. Right. Hello Glen, heard about the do, have you?

ROB: Look, I have arranged to look around. With the Committee.

EDDIE: Crossed wires then. 'Cos so have we. For the Gala night. Film premiere. Bands, turns, speakers. And me.

NEIL: You're the floor show, are you?

EDDIE: Oi, when we need a lock for the shithouse door we'll call you. Till then, bugger off. I'm rehearsing.

GLEN: Where's Sal?

EDDIE: Looking for you. Has been for weeks.

NEIL: She's been busy.

EDDIE: At El Vino's, eh? Funny she can work there but not here, innit?

NEIL: It's just short term. Getting shorter if you don't move.

GLEN: I just wanted to talk.

NEIL: Glen! We're working.

ROB: Look, Fiona will understand.

GLEN: Yeah, tell her I've turned Japanese.

NEIL: (*cutting her off*) Tell her she's ill. She'll be in tomorrow. Right. (*GLEN says nothing.*)

71

ROB: Right. Well, I'll let you get on. Best of luck with the do.

EDDIE: We'll send you an invite.

ROB: Look forward to it. Ciao for now. (*He goes.*)

NEIL: Aye, cio. (*follows him*)

EDDIE: Who's Ciao?

GLEN: I don't even know who tai chi is. (*Silence.*)

EDDIE: Reforming the band. Eddie and the Electricians. They haven't turned up.

(*SAL appears.*)

SAL: But look who has.

GLEN: Bad penny.

SAL: What the hell have you been doing, Glen?

GLEN: It's Tuesday. Must be tai-chi.

SAL: And what happens to the rest of the week?

GLEN: Everything. Business, leisure. Work, play. Wine bar, tai-chi. Tai-chi, wine bar. Wine bar, winebar, wine bar. Meetings, always meetings. And I never meet anyone.

SAL: You could meet me. Just call in.

GLEN: Oh no. Can't just call in. Have to make phone calls. Check diaries. Arrange. Meetings.

EDDIE: And this is what you look like after tai-chi, is it?

GLEN: It is if you run out.

EDDIE: So what now then, this film of yours, is it? (*Silence.*) Look, he won't come. Not Clem.

GLEN: Dad?

SAL: Thought he might do a soundtrack for us.

GLEN: No chance. He's gone into hiding with two ton of

72

oxo.

SAL: Eddie, you don't think you could —

EDDIE: I got nothing to say. It's history.

GLEN: I'm no talker, but I wouldn't mind a look.

SAL: Well. You might find something to say. (*She collects a cassette recorder from the equipment.*) Eddie, get the film going, will you.

EDDIE: Is this work or leisure?

SAL: Well, I'm not paying you.

EDDIE: Sodding leisure. Sick of the stuff. (*He makes his way to the box.*)

SAL: Now, I can offer you choc ice, but no wine.

GLEN: I only serve it, can't afford to drink it.

SAL: What's happened to Hitachi man?

GLEN: He's been wearing the wrong suit. (*Pause.*) He's alright now.

SAL: Yeah. Alright, Eddie?

EDDIE: I'm alright. Machine's a dinosaur.

SAL: You'll get on fine then.

         (*Film on screen. Long shot of valley community. Pans down to pithead.*)

SAL: There it is. What a tip. What did they used to call it?

GLEN: The blackhole.

SAL: Muckhole.

GLEN: Hellhole.

EDDIE: (*shouting from the box*) It was an 'ole whichever way you looked at it.

         (*CLEM'S voice from the darkness:*)

73

CLEM: The Big Sick. That's what we used to call it. 'Cos
           most of the buggers were on it. (*Shot of a group of
           men starting a shift.*) There's a rare, bloody sight,
           that fat git going to work. Billy Monthly, clocked
           on once a month, laid up in the chippy the rest of
           the time. Look at them all, they're all fat. Big, fat
           bastards squeezing down an 'ole. That's about the
           size of it.

SAL: Eddie, Eddie, hold it a minute.

           (*The picture freezes. We see CLEM. He has brought his
           own book.*)

EDDIE: Clem, mun. Afternoon at the pictures, eh. Brought
           your mac?

CLEM: No. Just this. (*holds up the book*)

SAL: What's that, Clem?

CLEM: History. And not some piss and fart of a film.

GLEN: It's more than that, Dad.

CLEM: Is it? Ten years of fat men cutting their own
           throats. Who wants that? No bugger. People want
           history, real history. (*He jabs a finger against the
           book.*) The hungry years, hungry men. That's what
           people want to know about.

SAL: Tell us then.

CLEM: It's all in here.

SAL: Well, tell us.

CLEM: (*He's absent-mindedly taken out an Oxo cube.*) It's all
           going down. Reams and years of it. Day by day.
           (*He is aware of them looking at the cube.*) Oxo. Your
           mother used to give it to me. In a flask. Warm me
           up. I have a quick sniff, try and get back there.
           Sometimes does the trick.

SAL: Wouldn't it be better if you drank it?

CLEM: Can't stand the bloody stuff. Never did. But she still gave it to me. Every bloody day. I told her but she didn't listen. Selective deafness that woman had.

GLEN: I wonder why.

SAL: So why've you come, Clem? Oxo not working? Stuck somewhere?

CLEM: I'm never stuck. It's there, all the time. I just — I just —

EDDIE: He just wanted a chat. Didn't you, Clem boy?

CLEM: Aye. Something like that.

SAL: Well, you come to the right place. (*She switches on the recorder.*) When you're ready, Ed.

(*The film restarts. Men entering the cage, waving, laughing.*)

CLEM: Aye, laugh you dull buggers.

GLEN: While they can.

(*The cage descends.*)

CLEM: Bye, bye, fatso. See you in a month.

GLEN: Or longer.

(*The picture moves to the pithead baths, empty. For the next minute the camera moves through the colliery: canteen, lamp room, winding house. All deserted.*)

CLEM: What's this then, miners' fortnight?

GLEN: Strike.

(*CLEM closes up almost physically for several moments.*)

SAL: Clem? Anything?

CLEM: Nothing. Nothing to say. Nothing to remember.

GLEN: Everything to remember. The longest year. And

the shortest.

CLEM: A non year. Rubbed out.

GLEN: You can't.

CLEM: I can. We all have. Haven't you noticed?

(*During the next exchange, there is a whole sequence of images from the strike: food convoys arriving, women unloading vans, men working in kitchens, children buttering bread, a room full of cans of baked beans with two women laughing uproariously, a woman giving a man a haircut, a man attempts the same on a woman; simple scenes full of laughter.*)

GLEN: Look at 'em. Lost.

CLEM: Knew exactly what we were doing.

GLEN: All lost for a while. Out of the kitchen.

CLEM: Writing our own sentence.

GLEN: Could sweat and smile then. We were doing something.

CLEM: But we pulled through. Came out the other side.

GLEN: Doesn't look much now though, does it?

CLEM: But you've got to dredge it all up again.

GLEN: Why do we look so different?

CLEM: Got where you want to be. Ought to be.

GLEN: Because we're laughing. You make it look as if we laughed for a year.

CLEM: In spite of all that. All that up there.

GLEN: Perhaps we did. Best year of my life.

(*The film moves on to several shots of EDDIE, NEIL, CLEM, SAL and GLEN on picket duty.*)

CLEM: Blot on my memory. (*He goes to walk out.*)

GLEN: No. (*She stops him physically.*) You were there, Dad. We all were. Together. (*He turns and looks.*)

(*Film of them all standing under a banner. It says "Women behind their men, not scabs behind their women." CLEM is talking directly to the camera. Though there is no soundtrack, suddenly there is a blank screen, a moment, then the film lurches back into life, then fast forward. A breakneck rollercoaster of images.*)

SAL: Eddie? Eddie, what do you think you're doing?

CLEM: Best part of the film.

SAL: Eddie! Eddie, pack it in.

(*The frame freezes. Three figures in blackened orange. TERRY appears at the back.*)

TERRY: Sorry, comrades. I had a neckful of that crap. Wanted to get to the bit where the heroes ride home, tall in the saddle, short in the arse. My old muckers. And here I am to join 'em. (*They just stare at him.*) Well come on, say welcome home, Terry. Welcome home, son.

CLEM: You little shit.

TERRY: That's no way to talk to your boy. (*looks at screen*) Our boys. All home.

CLEM: You're not my boy. No-one's boy.

EDDIE: (*still from the box*) He's mad. Had my arm up my back. He was mad when he went away and he's bloody madder now.

SAL: You. Hanging around the house. What are you playing at?

CLEM: Twisted. Come out that way. Been turning like a gimlet ever since.

GLEN: What are you doing here, Terry?

TERRY: Watching you. In your new world, your new house, your new, old wine bar.

CLEM: Not mine. Nothing to do with me. Wants a bomb under it.

TERRY: Eh, now that's mad talk. Thought it was books now, not bombs. Books, tinned salmon, hi-fis, cordless phones.

GLEN: You really have been sneaking around.

TERRY: Weighing you up.

CLEM: We've earned this.

TERRY: What did you think I did?

CLEM: Turned your sodding back. When it was hard you went. Buggered off with your stinking squaddie job in your stinking —

TERRY: Yes, my stinking, dirty job. Just like yours. Dirty job in different worlds. And now I'm back. In the same boat.

CLEM: Bugger off. Different planet you are, boy.

TERRY: I thought we were one big republic now. All fat and equal.

GLEN: What do you want, Terry?

TERRY: The same as you. A just reward.

CLEM: For bloody what? For shitting out. For living off our backs in your little khaki suit.

TERRY: And what did you do? Sat tight and dumb. And waited for the big pay day. The sell-out. How may pieces of silver was it?

CLEM: You cheeky young bastard.

(CLEM goes for him but TERRY twists him into an armlock and holds him double. The book drops to the floor.)

TERRY: Dirty jobs teach dirty tricks.

CLEM: Scab. Bastard little scab.

TERRY: Son, son, chip off the old block.

SAL: Leave him go.

TERRY: This man's dangerous, you know that.

EDDIE: You let him go, Terry. Now.

TERRY: Don't push it, boy, or I'll bust your fusebox.

(GLEN slaps him hard across the face.)

GLEN: You'll bust nothing, little brother.

(He instinctively lets him go.)

TERRY: Learnt that in the wine bar? Stick to books, old man.

(CLEM goes to pick up his book but TERRY gets to it first.)

CLEM: Give it to me.

TERRY: *(holding the book from him as if he were a child)* Now, now, don't snatch.

CLEM: I said give it to me.

TERRY: I thought you wanted us to see it.

CLEM: Just give it here, you brat.

SAL: Grow up Terry, give him the book.

TERRY: No, I think we should all have a look at the old man's service record.

CLEM: You keep your hands off it. *(makes another grab for it)*

TERRY: Come on Dad, heroes both, us. Let's see what you did in the war.

CLEM: Sharing nothing with you. *(He makes a final, violent lurch for the book and stumbles to the floor.)*

TERRY: You can share this. With your son.

(He opens the book at the first page, stares at it, then looks up. He turns the next page, then the next, quicker and again until he has flicked through the entire book.)

CLEM: *(quietly, without looking)* Have it back, please.

TERRY: Well, listen to this.

CLEM: Have it back, please.

TERRY: Nineteen fifty-seven.

CLEM: Shut up.

TERRY: Bill Haley comes to Cardiff.

CLEM: I said shut up.

TERRY: Nineteen fifty-eight, Eddie Cochran.

CLEM: Shut up.

TERRY: Fifty-nine, what a package: Gene Vincent, Chuck Berry, The Crickets.

CLEM: It's —

TERRY: And nineteen sixty, the Big Bopper hits Porth-cawl.

CLEM: It's not —

TERRY: Not what. Definitely not an 'ero's roll of bastard honour. So what the hell is it?

CLEM: It's not finished.

TERRY: Oh, it is, you can't add to that.

CLEM: There's more. The real bits. I haven't got to the real history yet.

TERRY: Working class hero. Working class wash out. *(He shoves the book at him.)*

CLEM: There's more. There is more. *(He starts to go, GLEN catches hold of him.)*

GLEN: There doesn't have to be, Dad. (*He shakes himself free, starts to go again.*) Come round the house, you haven't seen it. Have a look.

TERRY: Make sure you wipe your feet.

(*CLEM goes.*)

GLEN: I don't know what you want, Terry.

TERRY: And you don't know what you want either. Bad way.

(*She follows CLEM out.*)

SAL: Learnt a lot, haven't you Terry? How to destroy things.

TERRY: Only things that deserve it. Dangerous things. Or need it. Sick things. Sick or dangerous. They all get killed off. Know any? Let me know if you do. I'm feeling a bit spare.

(*He goes out.*)

EDDIE: Him. He's bloody both. Sick and dangerous. (*SAL is looking at the screen.*) Shall I run the film on? Or shall I wind it back? (*Silence.*) Sal? Back or forward? Sal? Which way? (*Three figures in blackened orange remain on the screen.*)

Celebration

(*The image goes and we are in the bright, white light of NEIL'S home. NEIL is talking down the phone. He has a new suit, new hairstyle and new voice. GLEN is somewhere off.*)

NEIL: Yes. A celebration. No, not some little piss up. I am talking proper stuff. Dinner. Yeah. No. No. No. Yeah, this is mega. No, my first sale, mun. Is that mega enough? Yeah, well I know there was the chubb lock but I don't really count that. This is the full system, the works. And it's down to you,

Rob boy. Yes it is, so you got to come round. Friday. Yeah, here of course. Glen is busting to practice on someone. What? Oh that Japanese thing, no that's history now. Forgotten. It was just a hiccup, a blip. That's right, a bit of a turn. She's — What's that? I sound different? Well I am. I bloody am. Down to you, pal. right, Friday then. Yeah, ciao to you. (*puts the phone down*)

GLEN: Who is Ciao?

NEIL: Dinner. Friday. Right? For four. No make it six. Not having no skimpy do here. Something appropriate, right. (*Silence.*) Glen, I'm serious. This is not just for me. It's for you as well. The both of us. It's important.

GLEN: Yes. I know it is, Neil.

NEIL: Right. So don't cock it up. (*he goes*)

GLEN: Something appropriate then.

(*cut to*)

(*Cinema blackness. A hi-tech Hitachi commercial comes on the screen. The image fades and is replaced by Japanese music. We are again in the bright, white light of NEIL'S home. There is a very low table set for dinner. Around it are scattered six cushions. ROB, FIONA, SAL, EDDIE and NEIL come in with drinks.*)

NEIL: And this is what we like to call the lounge diner.

EDDIE: Or the dining lounge.

NEIL: Well —

SAL: Piped music too.

EDDIE: Eh, I know this. They got this at Gin Hong's, I'm sure.

ROB: It's different.

NEIL: Yeah. (*shouting off*) Oi. Oi Glen, what's with this music? (*No answer. He turns back.*) It's a bit —

FIONA: Japanese.

(*Small, nervous laugh from NEIL.*)

ROB: You don't think she's turning —

NEIL: No chance. It's a joke, innit? She likes a laugh. Always — (*He clocks the table, stares at it as if he's never seen one before.*) She's laid the bloody coffee table for dinner.

ROB: Sure it's not another blip?

NEIL: No. (*shouting off*) Glen, what the hell are you doing up there? Everyone's here: Rob, Fiona, (*turning back to guests*) Sal and Eddie. You were a bit of a surprise too.

SAL: Bit of a shock for us. Never eaten with a councillor.

NEIL: I bet he's never eaten with an usherette.

EDDIE: It's murder mun, you have to find your food by torchlight. (*ROB is amused, SAL isn't.*) Tidy gaff you got here, Neil. Alright, mun.

ROB: Made his mark, hasn't he?

NEIL: Down to you, Rob. So let's get down to some serious celebrating.

EDDIE: Right. (*goes to drink*) What?

NEIL: What do you mean, what?

EDDIE: What we celebrating?

NEIL: Me, you pillock.

ROB: And his first major coup.

EDDIE: Oh right, you mean that chubb lock you sold. We heard about that. Well done.

NEIL: Eddie, I am talking mega sale, mega business. Full

83

	security system, everything, the complete works.
SAL:	Suit did the trick then.
NEIL:	It's not the suit darling. It's the three A's. (*Looks at ROB knowingly. SAL looks baffled, looks at FIONA.*)
FIONA:	Don't look at me. I think it's something to do with the Masons.
NEIL:	(*filling their glasses from a bottle of wine*) It's new skills, that's what it is. You've got to have them. New skills for a new age.
FIONA:	Well, let's drink to that then. New skills. And a new man.
NEIL:	Aye, and a new start. (*They drink. GLEN comes in complete with kimono and Japanese make-up. She virtually tiptoes her way to each guest and bows.*)
GLEN:	Sayonara. Sayonara. Sayonara. Sayonara.
NEIL:	What the hell are you doing?
GLEN:	Something appropriate. Sayonara.
NEIL:	What do you mean, sayonara?
EDDIE:	It's Japanese, innit?
NEIL:	I know its bloody Japanese.
FIONA:	I think we're having a Japanese meal, Neil.
GLEN:	(*nodding and smiling to her sweetly*) Sayonara.
FIONA:	There you are, right up your street, Neil. Couldn't be better.
ROB:	Yep, nothing like a bit of raw mackerel.
EDDIE:	What?
FIONA:	Rob.
NEIL:	For Christ's sake go and get yourself changed, you silly looking sod.

GLEN: Sayonara.

(He grabs hold of her and tries to take her to one side.)

NEIL: You're making a fool of yourself, Glen. And you're making a bloody dick out of me.

GLEN: Sayonara. *(She moves away.)*

NEIL: And stop saying that. *(She is collecting everyone's glasses.)* What you doing now?

GLEN: Sayonara. *(She bows and tiptoes to the table.)*

NEIL: What is the bloody woman doing? A joke's a joke but —

FIONA: Stop fussing Neil, it's a wonderful idea.

ROB: Yes, wish I'd brought my toga now.

FIONA: Kimono.

GLEN: Sake. *(She is standing before them with a tray of drinks in small china cups.)*

ROB: Ah sake, this will sort the sheep from the goats. This stuff killed more Japanese that two H-bombs, you know.

FIONA: Not the time for nuclear jokes, Rob.

ROB: It was a joke about sake.

GLEN: *(now standing beside the table)* Please to sit down.

NEIL: Where?

GLEN: Please. *(She gestures to the cushions.)*

NEIL: Someone has turned your sodding lights out. Look, no-one is squatting down at a bloody coffee table.

SAL: Are you alright, Glen?

EDDIE: This is the tai-chi, is it?

GLEN: Please. *(indicating to sit down)*

FIONA: (*moving towards the table*) Come on Neil, don't be a bore, think oriental.

NEIL: No way. I'll have mine standing up if I have to.

ROB: Ah well, when in Rome.

(*He sits down.*)

NEIL: I don't believe this.

(*GLEN goes over to ROB and begins to take his shoes off.*)

ROB: Um... is this really necessary?

NEIL: Glen! What the bloody hell — for god's sake, leave him alone.

GLEN: Hostess always takes guest's shoes.

NEIL: Since bloody when? Oh Jesus Christ.

(*ROB'S shoes are off now.*)

ROB: May as well enter the spirit I suppose. As long as I don't have to commit hara-kiri later on.

(*EDDIE has quickly taken his own shoes off and GLEN is now moving toward NEIL.*)

NEIL: Keep away. Put one hand on my foot and you'll have a mouthful of leather.

ROB: (*well into the sake*) Oh come on Neil, take your shoes off, let's all turn Japanese. (*FIONA throws him a look.*) No offence, Glen.

GLEN: (*bowing and smiling*) Sayonara. One moment. (*She turns to leave.*)

SAL: Do you want a hand, Glen?

GLEN: No problem. Wait and see. (*goes*)

NEIL: I don't want to see. It's probably a team of Sumo wrestlers.

FIONA: Neil. You work for Hitachi. They are a Japanese

firm.

NEIL: Well? Eddie was an electrician but he didn't dress up as a bloody battery.

ROB: You take their money, Neil. Only fair you should have a look at their culture. We all should.

SAL: Don't tell me, it's going to be the Hitachi Heritage Trail now, is it?

ROB: No. But I do have some news on that front. My own cause for celebration.

FIONA: Rob, it's Neil's night. Don't steal his thunder.

NEIL: Don't worry. Mata Hari's seen to that.

ROB: Perhaps later.

           (*Enter GLEN with a tray of food.*)

GLEN: Sushi, sashimo, nori maki.

NEIL: What is it?

FIONA: Looks wonderful, Glen. (*places tray on table*)

ROB: Now, are there any bull's testicles in there? I hear they're an aphrodisiac in Japan.

FIONA: Shut up, Rob.

EDDIE: Bull's testicles?

FIONA: He's joking.

ROB: It's true. Very catholic in their tastes the Nippon. Then again the Buddhist will eat nothing that has received the breath of life. Ah chopsticks. Nothing spared here. Pure grace and ceremony.

           (*He digs in with the chopsticks.*)

SAL: Glen? Are you joining us?

ROB: (*stopping suddenly*) Oh, sorry. Not thinking.

GLEN: No please, everyone.

(*She sits. Everyone begins to help themselves apart from NEIL who remains standing.*)

NEIL: Look, can't we be civilised and get some spoons?

ROB: There's an art to this, believe me. Small and subtle maybe, but no less an art. Once mastered never forgotten. (*He is filling two bowls and most of his lap.*) There you go. (*He hands NEIL a bowl and chopsticks.*) Crack that and you'll have Hitachi himself eating out of your hand.

(*They start to eat.*)

SAL: It's a bit —

EDDIE: Tricky.

ROB: Soon pick it up.

SAL: It's not easy.

NEIL: It's bloody impossible.

FIONA: Oh yes, it's very —

ROB: Well almost —

FIONA: Not quite —

ROB: What's the word?

EDDIE: (*holding a mouthful*) Raw. It's bloody raw.

ROB: Yes, that's it. Raw mackerel?

GLEN: Squid.

NEIL: (*spitting food back into the bowl*) You stupid, bloody woman. (*doorbell goes*)

GLEN: (*getting up*) Door.

NEIL: You stay where you are. It's probably a sumo kissogram. (*goes*)

ROB: (*valiantly chewing*) It's an acquired taste I suppose. We're just riddled with prejudices in this country. (*He starts picking at another bowl.*) Of course I'll try

	anything. Not too many qualms. As long as it's not moving. Is this... is this seaweed?
GLEN:	Yes. Nori Maki.
ROB:	Yes. Delicious.
	(*NEIL comes back.*)
NEIL:	Your father.
	(*CLEM follows.*)
CLEM:	You said come round. I've come.
NEIL:	Bit inconvenient really, Clem.
GLEN:	(*Getting up, the mask slipping for the first time.*) No. No, it's not.
CLEM:	Costume party, is it?
GLEN:	It's Japanese.
CLEM:	You've gone to town.
FIONA:	Nothing spared.
ROB:	Not even the feet.
GLEN:	This is Rob. And his wife, Fiona. Neighbours.
ROB:	Pleased to meet you.
GLEN:	Sit down. Have something to eat. I can cook you some chips.
CLEM:	No need. This'll do me. (*He sits down, piling a bowl with most of the food.*) How's leisure, Ed?
EDDIE:	Wearing me down. Know of any jobs?
CLEM:	Just my own. What's the crack then?
SAL:	We're celebrating.
CLEM:	'Course we are. (*He eats.*) What?
GLEN:	Neil.
CLEM:	Ah Mister Bettaware moved on to his second

suitcase, has he? Eh, you haven't got any free samples, have you? I could do with a new lock on the bog. (*He is now using the chopsticks with astonishing dexterity.*)

NEIL: I don't have a suitcase and I don't sell locks.

CLEM: You'll need a few on this place. Your place like this, Rob?

ROB: Similar.

NEIL: Rob's got one of the bigger houses.

CLEM: Thought as much. You're a bit of a big knob, aren't you? Too big for a poky hole like this.

ROB: Well — you're very handy with the old chopsticks, Mister —

CLEM: Clem. Malaya. National Service. Pick up anything with these.

EDDIE: You know that's raw, don't you Clem? Not cooked like.

CLEM: Eddie, I have had raw snake in my time, skinned and rubbed in monkey fat, raw dung beetle as fat as your fist, half barbecued fruit bat, and once, I was offered rat, pink and peeled and skewered on a stick. Drew the line there. I'd seen what he'd eaten first.

ROB: Ever had any bull's —

FIONA: You've obviously got some stories to tell.

GLEN: He's writing a book.

(*CLEM glares at her.*)

GLEN: Well... a journal.

ROB: War memoirs?

CLEM: Not the war you mean.

SAL: Underground. His life underground. The last

forty years.

ROB: We could do with you on the Heritage Committee. Tell me, are you using diaries or is it just memory?

EDDIE: He uses Oxo cubes. (*another CLEM glare*)

ROB: Oxo cubes?

EDDIE: Aye, he sniffs them and... and it all comes back to him.

ROB: Ah, sweet madelines.

CLEM: What?

FIONA: Proust's biscuits.

EDDIE: No, not even Jacob's cream crackers, only Oxo will do the trick.

FIONA: And does it? Do the trick.

(*CLEM just glares.*)

NEIL: 'Course it bloody doesn't. History of rock and roll is all he's got upstairs.

CLEM: Listen son, I have forgotten more than you'll ever know in a lifetime.

NEIL: There's nothing to know so there's nothing to forget.

FIONA: Careful Neil, you'll be treading on Rob's toes again.

NEIL: Rob knows what I mean. There's his half-baked history and there's —

SAL: The Councillor's heritage.

ROB: It's not my heritage. It's yours. So, I think we can all celebrate my piece of news.

FIONA: We're celebrating, Neil.

NEIL: You carry on, bottom of the bastard bill, me.

(*ROB gets to his feet.*)

FIONA: Oh for god's sake, just tell us, you don't have to make a speech.

ROB: (*Now quite drunk, he raises his hand.*) March. Nineteen ninety-five. (*He looks around expectantly.*)

EDDIE: That's next year.

ROB: Will be an auspicious date in this town's calendar. On that day the final piece of the Heritage jigsaw will slot into place. From the Cardiff Bay to the Milford Haven Marina, an historical tapestry will be finally sewn up. And we, this town, this community has the privilege of tying the last stitch. Right here on our own Heritage site we have been chosen to light the fuse that will blaze a trail across the country. TV, VIP attendance, a gala evening. A full blown, high profile party ceremony. What do you think of that then? (*He drinks. Silence.*) Well, I wasn't expecting any applause.

SAL: Where?

ROB: What do you mean where?

EDDIE: Where you holding it? This do.

ROB: The obvious place.

FIONA: The Institute.

ROB: In the cinema.

SAL: You can't.

ROB: Why not?

SAL: Because it's a cinema.

ROB: Well, not then it won't be. It'll have to be closed of course. Upgrading.

SAL: What?

ROB: I thought you'd be flattered. A major event in your own hall.

GLEN: Anyone for more sushi?

SAL: No, I'm sorry, you can't. We're there then. There's a date fixed. For us. The film. Our celebration.

EDDIE: That's right, it's a booking. Eddie and the Electricians.

SAL: It's all signed and sealed.

ROB: If it is, it'll have to be unsealed. There is a question of priority here.

SAL: I know. And it's ours.

GLEN: Or some sushimi. There's plenty —

SAL: Glen. They can't do this. They just can't. Tell them.

NEIL: You keep out of it. You've done enough damage for one night. Look, just show the bloody film again, that's all there is to it.

ROB: Yes. (*pause*) But not there. Once it closes, it remains closed. As a cinema. As does the Institute. Your film will have to be shown elsewhere.

SAL: That film was made there and it will be shown there. The Committee have agreed —

ROB: The Committee have agreed with the council. The Institute will be closed.

CLEM: Over my dead body.

ROB: Clem —

CLEM: Mister Lewis. And over Mister Lewis's dead body will that Institute be closed.

ROB: If you will let me finish, the Institute will be closed for renovation and rehabilitation.

SAL: As what?

ROB: As... as part of the Heritage Site. It will return to its original state. As a tourist attraction. Though there will be a lounge bar and the cinema will revert to a fully functional concert hall. Choirs, recitals and suchlike.

CLEM: Choirs and recitals! That's the place where Zorro made his mark, Brian Poole and the Tremeloes flooded the place in sweat, Eden Kane got booed off before he opened his gob.

ROB: Yes, well I'm not sure what visitors will make of that version of history.

CLEM: It's what we made of it, you jumped up little snotrag.

GLEN: Dad.

SAL: Not what ponces like you invent for us.

GLEN: Sal!

FIONA: Look, they're just trying to breath some life back into this place.

SAL: Yes, but they got to kill us off first. Him. Me.

ROB: This scheme will change the face of the whole region.

SAL: Let's all change our faces.

ROB: It will revitalise and re-energise —

SAL: Your wife's wine bar.

ROB: Communities that are dying on their feet.

SAL: Bring out your dead.

ROB: And this public launch is a unique opportunity —

SAL: To line your stinking pockets.

ROB: To heighten this area's profile and raise the public's consciousness of what is a moribund —

CLEM: What's the boy talking about?

ROB: Regeneration. That's what. And we won't be deflected from it. Not by films, old men, women or any other skeletons from nineteen eighty-four. March, nineteen ninety-five. We'll be there. With you or without you.

SAL: With us. And the film.

ROB: For god's sake, will someone tell the bloody woman!

(*Silence.*)

FIONA: It is cut and dried I'm afraid. All booked, right down to the speaker.

SAL: Who?

ROB: Yes, well now we're talking, aren't we? We are talking a high profile name. Perhaps now you'll understand that this is not some little jamboree. It's a platform. A springboard for the future.

SAL: Who?

ROB: That's something I can't divulge at —

SAL: He's speaking for us, isn't he? About our future.

ROB: I couldn't possibly —

CLEM: In our hall.

ROB: It's not really —

FIONA: For god's sake, stop pissing about. It's Terry Hamilton.

(*Pause.*)

EDDIE: He's a disc jockey, inne?

ROB: He's a pillar of the party.

CLEM: He's a pillock.

ROB: He's a respected figure.

EDDIE: He does that chat show.

ROB: He's a Member of Parliament.

SAL: He's a retard.

ROB: He's one of our leading thinkers.

SAL: He's a flaming dickhead.

ROB: He's the Secretary of State for Wales.

SAL: Exactly. We've got a retarded dickhead running the country.

            (*GLEN lets out a scream. Silence.*)

GLEN: Sorry. I'm sorry. I'm very sorry.

FIONA: No. It's us who should be sorry. All of us.

ROB: Yes. Sorry.

NEIL: Are you alright?

            (*The phone rings.*)

GLEN: Sorry. (*She gets up quickly to answer it. During the next exchange she says:*) Yes. Yes. Yes. Yes. Yes. Yes. Thank you.

NEIL: Sorry about that.

ROB: I blame the sake.

SAL: I don't.

ROB: Exactly, you haven't had enough.

FIONA: Shut up, both of you. (*NEIL is staring at GLEN.*) That might be for me. I left the number at the wine bar. They've probably run out of lager.

EDDIE: Send them the sake.

            (*GLEN puts the phone down.*)

GLEN: It was for you. The wine bar.

EDDIE: Can't find the corkscrew.

ROB: Send for Neil.

FIONA: Rob! What about the wine bar?

GLEN: There's a bomb.

FIONA: A what?

GLEN: A bomb. In the cellar.

ROB: A bomb in the cellar? What do you mean there's a
            bomb in the cellar?

NEIL: I have had enough of you tonight Glen, now stop
            dicking about.

FIONA: If it is a joke Glen, it's not funny.

GLEN: They haven't found it yet, but if they do they
            might have to... you know...

ROB: Jesus Christ, this is all I need.

FIONA: All you need!

ROB: We need, you need.

GLEN: They said you ought to be there. Just in case.

ROB: Right, right, I'll drive you over, come on.

FIONA: You can't — you've been — the sake.

ROB: Sod the sake, Japanese pisswater, I'm alright.

NEIL: Anything I can do, Rob?

ROB: No thank you Neil, you've done enough. I'll sort it
            out. (*turning on SAL*) if this is anything to do with
            you —

FIONA: Rob! Don't be so bloody stupid.

ROB: Sorry. Sorry everyone. Right.

FIONA: Yes. Sorry.

            (*They go. There is a silence then GLEN starts to
            giggle.*)

NEIL:	What's wrong with you? (*she giggles more*)
GLEN:	Dad always said they should put a bomb under it. (*The giggles turn to uncontrollable laughter.*)
NEIL:	Shut up. Shut up. Shut up. (*He hits her across the face.*) You stupid, selfish bitch.
CLEM:	(*on to his feet*) I'm not too old to —
NEIL:	Leave it there. My business. (*small move towards her*) You let me down, Glen. She let me down. (*goes out*)
CLEM:	He's got no business.
GLEN:	I'm alright, Dad. He's just —
SAL:	Not himself.

(*GLEN lets out a half sob.*)

CLEM:	No business. No business at all.
GLEN:	I know. I know he hasn't.
CLEM:	Look, I'll... I'll be around. You know where I am. Thanks for the chinky. (*He goes.*)
SAL:	Why don't you see how he is, Ed?
EDDIE:	It's alright. I'll hang on.
SAL:	Eddie. Please.
EDDIE:	Oh. Right. (*He gets up to go.*) He was out of order, Glen. Like everything else. (*He goes.*)
GLEN:	I want him back.
SAL:	Perhaps it's better if he —
GLEN:	No. Not him. Not that ugly thing who — (*She holds the side of her face.*) I want that man laughing on your film. I want him back. Laughing. How could he turn into that? How could all that on your film turn into this Welsh dream house, Japanese nightmare. Me, hostage in my own

house. Him, hijacked to another planet. Kidnapped. Hijacked. To here. (*looks at the debris of the meal*) Handed over the best part of our lives for this. A plate of raw fish.

SAL: We can get it back.

GLEN: No.

SAL: We can. If it's only for a day. If it's only to show 'em.

GLEN: We can't.

SAL: We can. We'll keep the hall open, we'll show the film, and you'll make the speech.

GLEN: 'Course I will. No problem. Easy meat. When?

SAL: After we've kidnapped him.

GLEN: Kidnapped who?

SAL: The retard.

GLEN: The retard.

SAL: Yes, the retard. Terry whathisface. We're going to kidnap the Secretary of State for Wales. (*GLEN opens her mouth, nothing comes out.*) And we'll get it back. It, him, everything. If it's only for a day.

GLEN: (*a growing laugh, hand to mouth, a swallow*) How?

(*The beginning of Roy Orbison's 'It's Over' "...your baby doesn't love you any more..."*)

99

Act Two

The Plan

(Faint light of juke box. First chords of 'Blue Bayou'. A gloomy light reveals EDDIE up a ladder, wearing his British Coal donkey jacket. He has his toolkit with him and he is working with a mass of wires. Terry stands beneath him.)

TERRY: I don't have to be here. I could be anywhere on this earth. I could be freezing my cobblers off in the polar wastes if I wanted to be. Or burning my arse away in the Gobi desert. Anywhere at all. No problem. If you want it, you do it. Just get up and go.

EDDIE: Piss off then.

TERRY: Look, what am I doing here?

EDDIE: All this is a mystery to you, innit?

TERRY: I been summoned that's all I know.

EDDIE: Wires. I'm talking wires.

TERRY: Listen sparkhead, you can stuff your cathodes where the sun don't shine.

EDDIE: See these two wires? I could plunge this hall into darkness with these. And those two, black out the whole of Wales.

TERRY: I don't give a toss, no-one summons me, right?

(EDDIE pulls the wires apart, the hall is plunged into darkness.)

TERRY: Sod off you nutter, stick 'em back on. Stick 'em on!

(The lights come back on. SAL and GLEN are now there.)

EDDIE: You haven't been summoned. You've been conscripted.

SAL: Your sister needs you.

GLEN: And you need us.

TERRY: What you on about?

EDDIE: Squaddie boy.

TERRY: Wrong man.

SAL: Bomber Lewis.

TERRY: What you trying to say?

SAL: Same as you. We all thought it needed a bomb under it.

TERRY: You can't stick that shit on me.

GLEN: We know you, Terry.

EDDIE: You're an 'eadcase. You'd do anything.

GLEN: To please Dad.

TERRY: I please myself.

SAL: You still can. And help us out.

TERRY: Why should I want to do that?

SAL: What else you got to do?

TERRY: Anything I want.

GLEN: What?

TERRY: Anything.

GLEN: What?

(silence)

EDDIE: All flights to the Gobi desert grounded?

SAL: You were right Terry, we're all in the same boat now.

TERRY: Have your eyes gone or something? I'm not in any bastard boat.

GLEN: But you could be.

SAL: Why did you do it, Terry?

TERRY: Do what?

EDDIE: Light up the sky with Fiona's wine bar.

SAL: Or try to.

GLEN: To get noticed? Well, we noticed. And we're all here.

TERRY: Cosy, innit? What next, blow this place up?

GLEN: No.

SAL: We want to keep it open.

TERRY: Oh right, a sit-in. Fuck off darling, you go and shove your placards.

SAL: No placards.

GLEN: No sit-ins.

EDDIE: An operation Ter. Manoeuvres.

TERRY: Are you going soft in the head?

EDDIE: This is soft. So soft it's simple.

TERRY: You're going to threaten to electrocute yourself. Go easy Ed, sounds like an offer they can't refuse.

SAL: We won't need threats.

EDDIE: Straight operation.

GLEN: All organised.

EDDIE: Clean as a whistle.

TERRY: What?

GLEN:	Kidnapping the Secretary of State.
EDDIE:	Hostage.
SAL:	For a day.
GLEN:	While we show the film.
SAL:	Make the speech.
GLEN:	Show them it's ours.
EDDIE:	Then we give him back.
SAL:	Point made.
TERRY:	This is a joke.
GLEN:	It's simple.
TERRY:	Simple. You are simple. Kidnap the Secretary of State — Jesus Christ, why stop there? Go on, shoot your load, knock off the Prime Minister while you're at it.
EDDIE:	He's not coming.
SAL:	We can do it.
TERRY:	What for? For this rotten hole. It's going, mun.
EDDIE:	We all are Terry boy, disappearing up our own arseholes.
GLEN:	(*straight at TERRY*) Well, I'm not.
TERRY:	OK, OK. How? This is not nicking jelly babies, this is carting off some bigwig. How you going to do it? "Excuse me Mister Secretary, would you mind locking yourself in the cupboard for five hours while we dick about in the hall? Oh, and could you hold this bread knife to your throat as well?" Sod off, you're moonwalking. You don't even know where he'll be. Or when. He'll have every twitch timetabled to the final second.
SAL:	We know.

GLEN: And so does Councillor Bentley. Our friend and neighbour. And does he love to talk.

SAL: About his pride and joy.

GLEN: The Heritage Project.

TERRY: There's such a thing as security, and it'll be crawling out of the woodwork.

GLEN: And it's called Neil.

SAL: Courtesy of Councillor Bentley.

GLEN: And he loves to talk as well.

TERRY: You've got to get in there first, for Christ's sake.

GLEN: You're looking at the catering corps.

. SAL: Courtesy of Councillor Bentley's wife.

GLEN: Come on Terry, your apron's waiting for you.

TERRY: I don't fit an apron.

EDDIE: Perfect cover for a headbanger like you.

SAL: Expert. We've got the theory, you've had the practice.

TERRY: This is fantasy island, it's gotta be. (*looks around*) Except you're sodding serious, aren't you? And what about him, the fuseless box, where does he fit in?

EDDIE: First there was light. (*He pulls the wires apart again. Blackout.*) Then there was bedlam. Know these circuits like the veins on my hand.

GLEN: Come on Terry, show the old man you can do something.

TERRY: Showed him. He didn't like it.

GLEN: Try something useful.

TERRY: Where is he anyway?

SAL: He's exactly where we want him to be.

(cut to)

(Light on CLEM on a bar stool near juke box.)

CLEM: Over my dead body. They'll have to close this place over Clem Lewis's dried-up carcass. They can stick me with the rest of the dummies in the museum. Clem Lewis, hunger striker, nineteen ninety-five. "Here's another blue-scarred stiffy for the disaster dump. They won't notice him under a million bastard others." There's more to us than bloody disasters, you know. This is the biggest bloody disaster. Nineteen ninety-five, the entire population of Wales was completely mummified. Well not me, not if I can help it. Not a morsel, not a sliver will pass my lips till they stop and take another look. See who lives here, sleeps, eats and drinks. Flesh and blood, not bastard waxworks. *(looks around the hall)* Paid for this a penny a week, now they'll charge a fiver a look. To squint and sniff at the corpse. Over Clem Lewis's dead body.

(cut to)

(ROB strides into the hall followed by NEIL in a security uniform.)

ROB: Smell that. *(breathes in deeply)* Paint.

NEIL: Aye. Tidy job.

ROB: No. A balls up. I don't want to smell paint. I want to smell roses. Nine o'clock and this hall should have been choked with them. It's ten fifteen and not a sniff.

NEIL: Roses?

ROB: That's right. No-one leaves this hall without a single rose. And a single purpose. Here and across the country.

NEIL: Aren't roses a bit —

105

ROB: What?

NEIL: Well. Old hat.

ROB: Out of yesterday, comes tomorrow. Remember that, Neil.

NEIL: Aye. Right.

ROB: And now I suggest you get on with your job.

NEIL: Yeah, well that's what I wanted to see you about.

ROB: I've gone to a lot of trouble to get you this. You said a day's work would be useful. So use it.

NEIL: It's not that. It's the uniform.

ROB: You're a security guard, what the hell did you expect?

NEIL: Well, I was thinking more of your plain clothes character, holding car doors and scanning upstairs windows.

ROB: Neil. There are jobs and there are positions. The Secretary of State has a position, I have got a position, the people who hold open car doors have got positions. You have got a job. And your job is to keep the nutters, loonies and wreckers out of this party. And for that you need a uniform.

NEIL: You mean bouncing.

ROB: I mean security. Cast iron security. And the only people I want in here are the people with positions.

NEIL: I'm only giving my —

ROB: Opinion? We're all of one opinion today and I want you to keep it that way. Perhaps you can start by making sure that old man of yours keeps his to himself.

NEIL: He's no problem. I got him under heavy guard.

	He can starve himself hollow, no-one will hear him belch.
ROB:	I hope not. This is a celebration of our heritage, the last thing we want is someone harping on about the past. The past is a foreign country Neil, they do things differently there. Usually badly. We've learnt the lesson, now let's close the book. Where the hell are those roses? (*He starts to go.*)
NEIL:	Shall I check the wine?
ROB:	What?
NEIL:	You check the roses, I check the wine.
ROB:	Let's just stick to our own jobs, shall we?
NEIL:	Positions.
ROB:	What?
NEIL:	Your position, my job.
ROB:	Don't get funny, Neil.
NEIL:	Me? Funny? Never.

(*They go, NEIL with a cursory glance at an upstairs window.*)

The Hit

(*Lights on FIONA and GLEN with the wine.*)

FIONA:	Exactly how casual is this casual labour you've arranged?
GLEN:	Completely uncasual. In fact it's completely committed.
FIONA:	To what?
GLEN:	Everything.
FIONA:	Yes, everything that undermines this whole event. I'm not totally green, Glen.

GLEN: They're all behind it.

FIONA: What?

GLEN: This do. And we all want jobs.

FIONA: Yes, and some of us want to keep them.

GLEN: Make or break, is it?

FIONA: I'll survive.

GLEN: What about Rob?

FIONA: He's a politician.

GLEN: We'll be alright then.

FIONA: Good. Just know your place and do your job. That goes for all of us. From the Secretary of State down to the lowest —

GLEN: Security guard.

FIONA: Look Glen, he didn't have to take it.

GLEN: He didn't have to offer it.

FIONA: No. But it's only temporary. Everyone knows that.

GLEN: I don't want him temporary.

FIONA: Yes. Well, you'll get back to where you were tomorrow.

GLEN: Yes. Where we were.

FIONA: The job in hand, now, alright?

(The Institute kitchen. SAL, EDDIE, and TERRY all dressed for the part. EDDIE is emptying a variety of olives into bowls. SAL is pouring out sherry. TERRY is throwing olives into the air and catching them in his mouth.)

TERRY: Bastard rich, innit? *(throws up an olive, catches it)* Come the revolution and we're in the catering corps.

EDDIE: It's not a revolution, it's work.

TERRY: Aye, in the catering corps. (*throws up another, catches it, chews*) Stuffed. Who the hell would stuff an olive?

EDDIE: Some Greek bugger.

TERRY: What sort of job is that for a grown man?

EDDIE: Useless.

TERRY: You'd know all about that, Eddie boy.

EDDIE: This is not useless, it's a job.

TERRY: Yeah, sorting out the stuffed from the unstuffed. Vital, mun.

EDDIE: I know what I'm doing, I'm not sure about you.

TERRY: I look after you useless buggers.

EDDIE: Dead end job.

TERRY: But not yesterday's. This is one off Eddie, then you'll go back to history. They'll mount you in the museum. The last electrician in Wales. One stuffed sparky.

SAL: Will you pack it in! Why the hell did we ask you, Terry?

TERRY: Professional among amateurs, that's why.

SAL: Right. So go through it then.

TERRY: We've been through it.

SAL: Go through it again.

TERRY: Someone getting nervous?

SAL: No. Getting professional. Six thirty.

TERRY: OK, let's get professional. Six thirty, depart kitchen.

EDDIE: And make way to the hall.

TERRY: Six thirty-five, circulate foyer.

EDDIE: Check out stage.

TERRY: Six forty-five, take up position in VIP lounge.

EDDIE: And set up in control room.

TERRY: Six fifty — can you button it for a minute?

EDDIE: I'm synchronising.

TERRY: Well try synchronising your brain to your mouth then we might stand a chance.

SAL: Get on with it.

TERRY: Fast as I can. Six fifty. Open doors, let in rabble. Grey suits, red roses. Wheel about like a buffet on castors. Sherry, olives and blah, blah, blah. Glide across to the man in question. Have an olive Sir, four at a time, why not, you fill your face. Six fifty, lose a castor, take a tumble. Sherry down the shirt front, olives in the turn-ups. Sorry sir, give you a quick wipe. Seven o'clock, dipstick kills the lights. Shit, bang, blackout. Head in groin, arm up his back, straight out the door. A swift tip-toe through the snooker hall. Wild, blind and legless. Down the stairs, through the bogs and smart as paint into the kitchen. Fusebox gives us light and wham, bam over to you. One roughed up, slightly soiled Secretary of State.

SAL: We said no rough stuff.

TERRY: He won't come by invitation.

SAL: You don't have to drag him by his haircut.

TERRY: Look, if you want to do it softly, I'll pack up my pinny and go home now.

SAL: Just bring him in one piece, that's all. Nothing missing.

TERRY: As long as Eddie kills the light and not himself.

No problem.

EDDIE: Skilled worker you're talking about, not some arm bender.

TERRY: We'll see who's got the skill.

SAL: Yes, we'll see who drops the olives first.

(TERRY throws up an olive, catches it, misses it, who knows? FIONA and GLEN come in.)

FIONA: Very impressive. What's your next trick?

EDDIE: He spits the stone in the sherry glass. *(Better still if he does.)*

FIONA: Glen, this is not what I call committed.

GLEN: No.

SAL: We've just been going over the schedule.

FIONA: You should know what you're doing by now.

SAL: We do.

TERRY: Aye. Serve up.

EDDIE: And shut up.

FIONA: You're not here to provide jokes. Just nuts and olives. Understood?

EDDIE: With you. Olive stuffers and olive eaters.

TERRY: And never the two shall meet.

GLEN: We all know our place.

SAL: Yes.

GLEN: And mine's here. In the kitchen.

FIONA: Keeping an eye on these two. Right, what have we got? Nuts, olives and laver bread canapes. I think we'll keep those back for the banquet. What do you think, Glen? *(no reply)* Glen, what do you think? About the laver bread?

GLEN: Cow muck, Neil calls it.

FIONA: Glen?

GLEN: What? Sorry.

FIONA: Are you alright?

GLEN: Yes. No. I was just thinking. The Secretary of State. He'll be here. In this very hall.

SAL: We've had bigger people than that here, Glen.

EDDIE: Aye, Billy Fury, Brian Poole, Tom Jones, before he was Tom Jones.

FIONA: Yes, but this is the Secretary of State. Now I know there's a lot of ill feeling about his, but that's in the past. Finished with. Now I won't be made a fool of. Because if this goes wrong we're all finished. And we all look fools. Now I'm not having that. Right.

            (*NEIL comes in.*)

NEIL: Security.

FIONA: Yes, we know who you are, Neil.

TERRY: It's Postman Pat.

NEIL: Look —

TERRY: Can we have a ride on your engine?

NEIL: Look! I am checking security. Right.

TERRY: Oh I'm secure. How about you Ed, are you secure?

EDDIE: Oh aye, tight as a duck's backside.

FIONA: What do you want, Neil?

NEIL: I'm securing the building. The Secretary of State is now on site and I'm checking all the personnel for any unauthorised personnel.

FIONA: I think you know everyone here, Neil.

NEIL: Yes, I do, and that's why I'm checking 'em. And I'll start with you. (*goes over to TERRY*) Come on AWOL, ID please.

TERRY: Oh, I'm definitely here, Neil. (*gets out card and shows him*) See, a bona fide black and white member of society.

NEIL: Watch this one, Mrs Bentley. He has a nasty habit of disappearing before your very eyes.

TERRY: Yes, but not up my own —

NEIL: Shut it. (*goes to EDDIE*) You surprise me, Eddie boy. Skilled man like you working as a menial. Whatever happened to leisure?

EDDIE: Knackers you mun, I got a doctor's note for it now. (*gives him his card*)

NEIL: Word in your ear. Don't lower yourself.

          (*looks at his card*)

EDDIE: I'll try not to, Neil.

NEIL: What's this?

EDDIE: My ID.

NEIL: Who are these other two on it?

EDDIE: Well, that's the top of Clem's head by there, and that's you pulling a face in the corner. Remember the TUC conference in Blackpool, that booth on the pier?

NEIL: You prat.

EDDIE: You don't remember.

NEIL: No. (*to SAL*) And what have you got for me? A shot of my family in Benidorm?

SAL: Don't be dull, Neil. It's Vienna or nowhere these days. (*hands him the card*) And that's nowhere.

NEIL: She's the one, Mrs Bentley. Danger. Watch her.

113

FIONA: I'm watching the time.

NEIL: One minute.

(*He stands in front of GLEN.*)

GLEN: What are you looking at me like that for?

NEIL: I'm waiting for your ID.

GLEN: I'm your wife.

NEIL: Are you authorised?

GLEN: I'm not sure. For better or worse, for richer or poorer, till death do us part. To love, cherish and obey. No, I'm not, am I? I'm sorry.

NEIL: Are you authorised to be in this —

FIONA: Neil, I think you're overstepping the mark.

(*He pulls GLEN to one side.*)

NEIL: Why are you getting involved with this pair?

GLEN: Why are you a security guard?

NEIL: I'm not. It's a one off. Now, I'm asking you Glen, don't let me down. Not again. Don't make me look like an idiot.

GLEN: Look at yourself, Neil. What are you doing?

NEIL: My job.

GLEN: And I'm doing mine. Perhaps we found our place.

FIONA: Can we get on now, Neil? Have we all been cleared?

NEIL: Mrs Bentley, I think you ought to know —

FIONA: I don't want to know. Today Neil, there are those who think and there are those —

NEIL: Who wear the uniforms. Right?

FIONA: That's not what I was going to say.

NEIL: But it's what you were thinking. All wind and piss upstairs that's me, innit? Well you might think I know nothing but I know this pair. Opposite poles they might be, but stick 'em together, under one roof, you got a time bomb. Note the words, Mrs Bentley. Time bomb.

FIONA: I am surrounded by time bombs. You, this pair, that clown upstairs trying to starve himself. What's wrong with you all?

NEIL: Only trying to help, Fiona. That's all.

FIONA: Right. Well, why don't you start by checking our hunger striker's ID. Something to keep him occupied.

TERRY: Try giving him a laver bread canape.

FIONA: I am getting sick of your jokes.

TERRY: Straight up mun, laver bread, he can't resist it.

SAL: Shut up, Terry.

(*FIONA stares at TERRY for a moment.*)

FIONA: Right. Let's start as we mean to go on. One time bomb about to be detonated. (*She picks up the tray of canapes.*) Neil, get up to that bar and make sure no-one wanders in. Apart from me.

GLEN: What are you doing?

FIONA: Taking care of the time bombs. You do the same down here. Neil, the bar.

(*She goes.*)

NEIL: I'll be double-checking later.

(*follows her*)

TERRY: That's got rid of her. Just down to us now.

GLEN: Not me.

TERRY: What?

GLEN: It's not down to me. I can't do it. Sorry.

SAL: Can't do what?

GLEN: Any of it, can't do any of it.

TERRY: Well, let's all piss off then. I'm not wearing this pinny for nothing.

SAL: Shut up. Why can't you do it?

GLEN: It's wrong.

SAL: We know it's wrong, that's why we're doing it.

GLEN: It's not our place.

SAL: Our place. What the hell's our place?

GLEN: He's the Secretary of State, that's his place. Neil, he's a security guard, that's his. And me, I'm in the kitchen, and that's my place.

SAL: You think so? You in a pinny and Neil in a uniform.

GLEN: Yes. Perhaps. And now I'm cheating on him, lying to him. Using him.

SAL: He has been using you for months.

GLEN: It's not his fault.

SAL: And it's not yours.

GLEN: Someone's though. Someone's brought him here, given him the scent for some damn thing. He's forgotten what it is. Like Clem, memory shot to pieces. Perhaps he found it, perhaps this is his place.

TERRY: Aye, down to the ground. The museum screw.

EDDIE: No. That's not Neil. He's more, mun. Like she's more than an usherette and you're more than a poxy wine waiter.

TERRY: And you're more than Eddie and the Electricians.

116

EDDIE: They're dead. But I'm still here. Doing the wiring. My job. Now you can do what you flaming like but I'm getting on with it. Let's see if you're more than an armbender. It's six thirty.

TERRY: Depart kitchen.

GLEN: I'm not the one.

SAL: So what do you do? Leave it to someone else. Terry. Eddie. Or just let Rob get on with it.

EDDIE: On contract now, you can't break it.

TERRY: With you or without you, sister.

SAL: You think Rob knows Neil's place.

GLEN: He doesn't know his own.

TERRY: Six thirty-two.

EDDIE: (*to GLEN*) Remember to open the door. For the light. It's on a different circuit.

SAL: All those upstairs. They've all come here to forget, Glen. We're here to remember.

EDDIE: So don't forget the door.

TERRY: Simple.

(*They go, leaving GLEN alone.*)

GLEN: Simple. Don't forget.

(*cut to*)

(*Lights up on CLEM. He is singing along to the juke box. 'Only the Lonely.'*)

CLEM: Roy Orbison. He was a funny looking bugger. White face, black eyes, that's all you could see from the back of the Capitol. Rocking Berries, they were there too. Hard buggers they were. Fought the bouncers half way through 'He's Back in Town'. And Petula Clark. Jesus Christ, what the hell was I doing seeing that silly bitch. Waiting for the Big O. Dreaming. In dreams. Biggest, bastard dreams you could imagine. In here on a Saturday night. Eight pints then into a bottle of pale ale. (*He sings into an imaginary beer bottle, the intro to 'In Dreams'.*) "A candy coloured clown they call the sandman, tiptoes to my room every night. Just sprinkle stardust and he whispers, go to sleep. Everything is alright..."

(*FIONA comes in, bearing gifts.*)

FIONA: Roy Orbison, the Capitol, 1963.

CLEM: No. Clem Lewis, The Institute, 1995.

FIONA: Well, it did sound like Roy —

CLEM: What do you know about Roy Orbison?

FIONA: My father —

CLEM: Didn't know him. Not from round here, was he? Nor you.

FIONA: No.

CLEM: Still, never turned our back on strangers. Long as they fit in with us. Not us with them.

FIONA: When in Rome —

CLEM: Do as the Romans, when in Ponty, keep your bloody head down. What do you want?

FIONA: I thought you might like some —

CLEM: Bribery and corruption? No thanks, I'm full to the neck with it. What is it?

FIONA: It's laver bread.

CLEM: Bloody seaweed again. Don't people eat anything decent these days?

FIONA: I thought you might like something traditional. My mother used to cook it in —

CLEM: I know. Bacon fat. Bloody disgusting. Who

118

dreamed up that dog mess I don't know. I suppose that's our staple diet from now on, is it? Well not me, and I'm not joining any sodding choir either.

FIONA: Perhaps I could get you something else.

CLEM: Nothing. I am eating nothing. Not till you, your husband and that party of stuffed suits has vacated my club.

FIONA: Mr Lewis, that's not going to happen.

CLEM: You're talking to a dead man then. Forget the food, order the flowers.

FIONA: Is this really worth making yourself ill for?

CLEM: Who mentioned ill? Dead I said.

FIONA: Mr Lewis. Clem. This place will be more alive than it's ever been. And you'll still have your bar. Exactly as it was eighty years ago.

CLEM: Does that mean you'll be getting shut of the juke box?

FIONA: Well, of course.

CLEM: You can stuff it then. That is the best juke box outside of America. Definite.

FIONA: Aren't you getting a little old for juke boxes?

CLEM: Never. I was brought up with juke boxes, educated by juke boxes. In fact if the truth were known I did most of my conceiving over the top of a bloody juke box. He who is tired of juke boxes —

FIONA: Is tired of life?

CLEM: Right, right. Bloody right.

(*A moment's silence on this rare point of agreement.*)

FIONA: You're writing a book, aren't you? History.

CLEM: Trying.

FIONA: Why?

CLEM: Because it's disappearing, you daft cow. And I got to get it down. My history. If that is history.

FIONA: It comes in all shapes and sizes.

CLEM: Not mine. It doesn't fit, does it? Not proper, not the real thing.

FIONA: Your memories are just as valid as any of this.

CLEM: You can put the soft soap away now, 'cos I'm no soft socialist.

FIONA: No soft soap. I'm just saying your story can still be told. Here in this place.

CLEM: I'm here telling it. We all are. Every day. So why don't you go and tell your old man to clean his ears out and listen.

(*sudden darkness*)

FIONA: What's that?

CLEM: The dark.

FIONA: Well, what's happened?

CLEM: The lights have gone out, you silly bitch, what do you think?

(*cut to*)

(*There is a dull thud. Still dark.*)

EDDIE: Here. It's over here.

TERRY: Where's the light?

EDDIE: It's not on.

TERRY: Brilliant. You've screwed it, haven't you? You nailbender.

EDDIE: It's not me, it's her in there, she hasn't switched it on.

TERRY: Wet necked civvies. I hate you bastards. Out the way. Out the way.

EDDIE: I am out the way. There's the sodding door.

TERRY: Get in there. On the floor. Floor! Down.

SAL: Where's the light?

TERRY: Oh Jesus Christ, I've eaten it, alright!

SAL: Well where's Glen? Glen. Where's the switch?

EDDIE: Shall I light a match?

TERRY: What do you think this is, a fucking Dire Straits concert?

SAL: A torch, we need a torch.

(*a strangulated voice:*)

TERRY: Wrap up or I'll set fire to your head and use that.

SAL: For god's sake Eddie, find the light. Do something.

(*The light comes on. GLEN is just standing there. TERRY is kneeling on a man's back. The man has a cloth wrapped around his head.*)

TERRY: Where the hell have you been?

GLEN: You're early.

TERRY: Oh I'm sorry, we'll go back and do a couple of laps of the building, shall we?

SAL: Get him in a chair.

TERRY: Come on Mister Secretary, where's your dignity?

(*dumps him in a chair, ties his hands to the back of it*)

SAL: What have you got on his face?

TERRY: My pinny. Wouldn't stop squawking would he, like a buggered parrot.

SAL: Take it off.

GLEN: He'll know who we are.

SAL: Glen, in one hour, eight hundred people are going to know who you are. Or are you going to speak with a pinnny on your head?

EDDIE: Got to show 'em as well as tell 'em.

TERRY: Listen to him, the shadow in the dark.

SAL: You've done your bit Ed, leave it to us.

EDDIE: Aye, I have done my bit. And without it he wouldn't be here. (*directly to TERRY*) Vital, right? As vital as any of you. Still am too. Your film's not going to run on gas, is it?

SAL: Sorry. It's easy to forget.

EDDIE: Right.

GLEN: Right. Better take it off then.

(*EDDIE unties the pinny. A reddened ROB BENTLEY is revealed. They stare at him. He stares at them.*)

ROB: You bloody lunatics.

SAL: That's not the Secretary of State.

TERRY: Innit?

EDDIE: That's Glen's next door neighbour.

GLEN: Hello, Rob.

(*cut to*)

(*The bar. A match is struck and we see the faces of CLEM and FIONA.*)

FIONA: I think we should try and make our way out.

CLEM: Go ahead. But I'm not budging and you're blind as a bat.

FIONA: Yes, but I really should be there.

CLEM: Can't celebrate in the dark, can they? Sit tight.

Wait.

(*He strikes another match.*)

CLEM: Eight left.

FIONA: Fingers or matches?

CLEM: Both.

FIONA: How are they? The fingers.

CLEM: Got asbestos tips. How's the eyes?

FIONA: Getting used to it.

CLEM: You do. All the different bits of dark. We got different words for it underground. Like the Eskimoes and snow. This is just a smidge of dark, see. Then you get your plain dark, your bloody dark, your effing dark and your Jesus Christ, who put that sodding wall there.

FIONA: Black is black to me. (*The match goes out.*)

CLEM: Be simple then, wouldn't it? (*strikes another match*) Couldn't do this underground. Blow us both to buggery.

FIONA: Do you miss it?

CLEM: Oh aye. The gas, the black, the cold, the wet. Miss all that.

FIONA: You're glad to be out of it then?

CLEM: Mrs Bentley, I was part of things. Crucial. Understand? (*The match goes out.*) They're missing someone crucial here as well. Like a sodding electrician.

FIONA: You could still be part of things you know, part of this place.

CLEM: I am part of this place.

FIONA: I know, I know. But you can be part of its future as well. It can't stay like it is. And neither can you.

CLEM: A new man, eh?

FIONA: Yes.

CLEM: Like Neil?

FIONA: Well —

CLEM: Well what?

FIONA: Well at least he's trying.

CLEM: Aye, he'll try it all, he will. None of it bastard fits.

FIONA: Yet.

CLEM: He won't. And I won't. Fit into your scheme, your project or whatever you damn well call it. Jesus Christ, doesn't anyone have dreams anymore? Do you, Mrs Bentley?

FIONA: Well, I have ambitions I suppose.

CLEM: What are they?

FIONA: Well, lots of things.

CLEM: What?

FIONA: Well. Security, success, independence.

CLEM: I'm talking about dreams, for god's sake. Big bastard dreams, not your poxy little desires. I used to have 'em, gave 'em up. Settled for second best. It's not even that, is it? It's some other bugger's project. Someone else's ambition. Is that what we settled for, Mrs Bentley?

(*She says nothing.*)

(*NEIL bursts in carrying a torch.*)

NEIL: You bloody provocateur! Bloody guerrilla, bloody decoy, bloody bastard!

CLEM: Problem?

NEIL: You're the fucking problem.

FIONA: Neil!

NEIL: Sorry. But it's him. Him and his bloody, terrorist family.

CLEM: Terrible, yes, but terrorist, definitely not.

NEIL: Don't get wide-eyed with me, sitting up here like some starving buddha while all hell breaks loose down below.

FIONA: What hell? What terrorist? What are you talking about, Neil?

NEIL: Mrs Bentley, this mental defect and his retarded offspring have kidnapped the Secretary of State. In broad daylight, while the lights were out.

CLEM: I haven't moved for days.

NEIL: Exactly. Decoy. Bloody decoy.

FIONA: Neil, you're not talking sense. The Secretary of State has been kidnapped?

NEIL: No. Not exactly.

FIONA: He either has or he hasn't been.

NEIL: He hasn't.

FIONA: So what's the fuss about?

NEIL: They've kidnapped Rob instead.

FIONA: Rob?

NEIL: Aye.

FIONA: Why the hell have they kidnapped Rob?

NEIL: I don't think they meant to. They all look the same, don't they? And it was dark.

FIONA: I'm not following any of this.

NEIL: Ask him, he's behind it all.

CLEM: I'm behind nothing.

FIONA: Will you please stop it and explain to me exactly
            what is going on.

NEIL: Right. The lights go out, don't they? So I make my
            way to the hall and there's bedlam. Grey suits, red
            roses, green olives. All over the shop. Eight
            hundred bigwigs without a bastard clue in their
            heads. Except Rob. But he wasn't there. Which is
            how we noticed he was missing. Then we see it on
            the screen. "We have your Secretary of State. Give
            us back our hall." Except they haven't got him.
            They've got Rob.

FIONA: Oh, fuck.

            (*cut to*)

            (*an open-mouthed ROB*)

ROB: What the hell are you doing?

SAL: You've kidnapped her next door neighbour. A
            poxy little Councillor.

ROB: I'm not a poxy little —

SAL: What did you kidnap him for?

TERRY: It wasn't deliberate.

SAL: Accident then, was it?

TERRY: No.

SAL: What then? This one gave himself up? Please,
            please, take me, let me be your prisoner.

TERRY: They all looked the same, didn't they?

SAL: All looked the — you amateur, bloody amateur.

EDDIE: Arm bender.

TERRY: Shut it, you.

EDDIE: Skilled man.

TERRY: I said shut it.

EDDIE: Skilled bouncer more like.

TERRY: You bastard little wirehead.

            (*He goes for him but is stopped by a sudden yell from ROB.*)

ROB: I am not a poxy little Councillor! (*They all stare at him.*) As you will find out soon enough.

SAL: We've blown it. We've blown it all. What the hell are we going to do with him?

ROB: You're going to untie me, that's what, stop this charade and let me get on with my job.

TERRY: Piss off.

EDDIE: We can't keep him here.

TERRY: Why not?

SAL: He's her next door neighbour.

EDDIE: Not much point kidnapping someone's next door neighbour.

ROB: I'm not someone's next door neighbour, I am a leading Councillor who happens to be in charge of this whole operation. (*They look at one another.*) This is ridiculous. Now listen, I'm getting up, you're stepping aside and I'm walking out. Alright? (*They say nothing. He gets up, the chair comes with him, he sits back down again.*) Will you please untie me? Now. (*nothing*) Right. OK. Fine. (*he calls out*) Hello. Hello there. In here. The kitchen. Hello. Somebody.

            (*Silence.*)

EDDIE: Quiet, innit?

ROB: (*at the top of his voice*) Help! Help! Somebody please. In the kitchen. Anybody. Can someone please come and sort these bastards out. Help! Help!

SAL: There's no need for that. Councillor, there's no
           need for — Eddie, shut him up.

EDDIE: How?

SAL: I don't know, stick your hand on his mouth.

EDDIE: Sod off.

SAL: Terry, will you stop him. Mister Bentley, will you
           please shut up? Terry, do something.

           (*TERRY smacks him straight in the mouth, knocking
           him and the chair over. ROB shuts up, as does
           everyone else.*)

ROB: He hit me.

SAL: You hit him.

ROB: You've broken my crown. You've broken my
           bloody crown.

SAL: What did you hit him for?

TERRY: Negotiations ended.

EDDIE: Bastard psycho.

TERRY: Bastard skilled man, right.

SAL: You weren't supposed to hit him. That wasn't the
           plan.

ROB: I'll have you for this. Abduction, assault, GBH, I'll
           throw the bloody book at you.

SAL: Jesus Christ what a mess, what a bloody mess.

EDDIE: Bit of a balls up.

           (*SAL takes GLEN to one side.*)

SAL: What the hell are we going to do?

GLEN: Nothing.

SAL: Nothing?

GLEN: Nothing.

SAL: Glen. Wake up. It's not working. We are stuck with a dead fish.

GLEN: Nothing changes. Just the name. Like Terry says, they all look the same. All the way down the line. They can even change the parties but the faces stay the same. Same suits, same faces. (*turning to ROB*) And I know this one.

ROB: Glen, if you are having one of your funny turns...

GLEN: I have turned enough.

EDDIE: But he's just a poxy little —

GLEN: Leading Councillor. Isn't that right?

ROB: Well, yes.

GLEN: In charge of this whole operation?

ROB: Well —

EDDIE: Are you?

ROB: Yes.

GLEN: And it can't go on without you?

ROB: Well, I wouldn't —

GLEN: Can it?

ROB: No. I don't suppose —

GLEN: See. Nothing changes. Except perhaps for the better.

SAL: Glen, everything's changed. We've kidnapped a bloody nobody. It's over. Finished.

EDDIE: No. It's not finished. I've done the wiring but not the job. A job half done.

SAL: I'm not hearing this. Eddie, watch my lips. There is no point in going on.

EDDIE: There's been no point to me for bastard months. Today's different. I don't want to stop.

SAL: Well, I'm stopping it right now. We are leaving it there.

EDDIE: No. Done that before. Coal left at the face. Sealed over. It's not right. Should see it come up. Wheels turning. A good day's work. Same with your film. Should see it through.

SAL: Since when did you give a toss about my film?

EDDIE: I don't. But it's all part of it. Lights off, show the film, lights on. So I want to see it through.

ROB: All this for a film?

SAL: Yes. All for a cheap old film. That's bloody all.

GLEN: No.

SAL: It is. That's why we're here. All for a crappy bit of film.

GLEN: Well, if that's what you think then perhaps you'd better bugger off. Leave us to it.

SAL: What?

GLEN: Bugger off. Go on. Make another film for no-one to see.

SAL: I made it for me.

GLEN: Did you? What's it doing here then?

(*SAL says nothing.*)

EDDIE: So we can all watch it. Right to the end.

GLEN: Right to the end this time, Sal.

TERRY: Or slink off home again, banners between our legs.

ROB: You can. I won't say a word. Carry on as normal.

SAL: No. Done that before, haven't we?

GLEN: Yes we have, Sal. Not this time.

EDDIE: Right. Good day's work this time.

SAL: Depends.

GLEN: On what?

SAL: How indispensable is your next door neighbour?

EDDIE: Well, how indispensable are you?

ROB: I've told you, I'm running the operation and no-one will lift a finger while I'm surrounded by — look, it is quite clear that they are giving this some serious thought.

EDDIE: Are they?

ROB: Obviously.

SAL: Come on Councillor, what are they thinking out there?

            (*nothing*)

TERRY: I'll tell you what they're thinking. They're thinking, well thank shit for that, we've got rid of him at last. Indispensable, yeah, like a spare prick at a wedding.

GLEN: Well?

ROB: Well —

TERRY: He knows. They don't give a toss. Look at the time and not a squeak from his precious party. You're forgotten matey, a lost cause. Missing presumed dead.

ROB: I don't think you know the party very well.

TERRY   I know they can't think much of you.

EDDIE: So what do we do?

TERRY: We give them something else to think about.

            (*cut to*)

            (*CLEM*)

131

CLEM: What speech?

NEIL: Ask your bloody daughter, she's the one making it.

CLEM: She's your bloody wife.

NEIL: No wife of mine makes sodding speeches. She gets that from you.

CLEM: Nothing to do with me. This is my protest.

NEIL: This is your fault.

CLEM: This is my moment.

FIONA: This is my chance.

            (*silence*)

CLEM: We been buggered, Mrs Bentley. Buggered by a kidnap. A bloody kidnap. This is history, innit? Here and now.

NEIL: It is not history, it is a breakdown in security. And if it's this idiot's fault, Mrs Bentley, I have to say that you are the one to blame.

FIONA: What?

NEIL: I warned you, didn't I? About those mad buggers. Time bombs. And here they are ticking away while everyone runs about like headless chickens.

FIONA: There's only one headless chicken and it's you. So why don't you get your brain in place and do something.

NEIL: I am. I'm questioning him.

CLEM: Wrong man.

NEIL: You're behind it.

CLEM: They're behind it, Neil boy. Two soft boys and couple of daft tarts. (*slight laugh*) Holding the new world to ransom. Some joke.

NEIL: Oh yes, I am laughing my cock off, I am. Well this is jobs on the line and there'll be no bugger laughing when they've all fallen — what did you say?

CLEM: I said some joke.

NEIL: No, before, before. Two soft boys and a couple of daft tarts. That's all they are. Soft and daft. Nothing else. Nothing to worry about. So carry on, that's what I say. Fix the lights and on with the show. As if they weren't there.

FIONA: And what about Rob?

NEIL: No-one will miss him. Well they didn't, did they? Mountain out of a hill of shit this is. And those plain clothed pillocks can't see it. But I'm just the man to tell 'em.

CLEM: Before they tread in it.

NEIL: Dead on, Clem boy. This is where I make my mark. I'm owed this, isn't that right, Fiona?

FIONA: I think you probably are, Neil.

NEIL: My moment, Clem. You watch.

(*He goes, leaving the other two in darkness.*)

FIONA: We all want to be stars, don't we? For fifteen minutes.

CLEM: But what about the rest of the time?

(*cut to*)

(*ROB. TERRY is pointing a gun at his head.*)

ROB: Jesus Christ.

SAL: What the hell are you doing?

TERRY: I'm pointing a gun at his head.

ROB: Oh fucking hell.

SAL: Terry, put it away, now. (*He does nothing.*) Terry!

TERRY: The cooks are threatening the Councillor. Big deal. They'll probably think he'll end up in a cake mix. But if they think we might blow his brains out. Different movie.

ROB: Jesus Christ, can you stop this lunatic please?

EDDIE: Come on Terry, don't be mad.

TERRY: Don't worry, Rob. Skilled man, me.

SAL: Glen, we don't want this.

(*GLEN says nothing.*)

TERRY: She knows, see. Why I'm here. Why you asked me. To do the things you can't do. Can't even think about. The dirty work. Now, Eddie's done his bit, so let me get on with mine so you can do your bit. (*SAL just stares at him.*) Hard at the front, innit?

(*SAL looks to EDDIE then to GLEN.*)

GLEN: Means to an end. That's all.

SAL: That's all. Well Councillor, I only hope they do care something about you. For all our sakes.

EDDIE: What do we do now then? Phone 'em up?

TERRY: No. But he can. Straight from the horse's mouth. (*He jabs the gun against the side of ROB'S mouth.*)

ROB: You're happy with this, are you? What this madman is doing. Because you know what it is. It's terrorism. And act of outright terrorism.

GLEN: No.

ROB: Oh, what do you call it then?

GLEN: Revenge.

ROB: Oh, even better. Neil's going to be very proud of you, isn't he?

GLEN: Pride's all gone from him. You took that as well. Not the Secretary of State. You. Took Neil. And I don't think I can get him back.

ROB: I have taken nothing. Given, that's all I've done. That's what this whole thing is about. Giving something back.

SAL: But what if we don't want it?

(He looks at them, shakes his head in disbelief.)

TERRY: Time to phone, Councillor. Untie him, Eddie.

(He presses the gun a little harder. ROB lets out a groan.)

TERRY: Just a warning. Like the wine bar.

ROB: What?

TERRY: That was alright, wannit? Controlled threat.

ROB: You? Why?

TERRY: My old man didn't like wine bars.

ROB: My old man didn't like a lot of things, it didn't mean I had to blow them up.

TERRY: He thinks I'm a useless sod, an uncaring bastard. We all have our uses. And we all care. About something. I wonder if those out there do. *(He is now untied.)* Time to find out. Phone 'em.

ROB: Glen. You really don't want to go along with this. You can stop now and nothing more will be said. I've got influence. I know it wasn't you who hatched this up. I know that, Glen.

GLEN: No, it wasn't. It was all of us. And we didn't hatch it up, we dreamed it up. Understand?

ROB: No. I don't. I honestly don't.

SAL: That's the problem.

GLEN: Phone 'em.

(She picks up the phone and holds it out to him.)

ROB: On your heads. On your stupid, ungrateful heads. *(He snatches the phone.)* Any specific message?

TERRY: Just tell 'em to do what we want. *(He lowers the gun to ROB'S groin.)* Or they'll be picking your privates out of the lampshade.

(ROB dials. Waits.)

SAL: Is it ringing?

ROB: 'Course it's ringing. *(waits)* Come on, answer the damn thing.

TERRY: They really think about you, don't they?

EDDIE: Perhaps they can't find the phone in the dark.

ROB: And whose bloody fault would that be? For god's sake pick the phone up, you idle bastards.

EDDIE: Wrong number perhaps.

ROB: Will you please shut up? Answer it. Answer it!

(NEIL'S voice from outside.)

NEIL: Oi. Open this door or I'm breaking it down.

(ROB looks at the door, then at the gun.)

ROB: No! Stay where you are, for Christ's sake.

NEIL: Don't worry Rob, I've sorted it out. No sweat.

TERRY: You'll see more than sweat if you touch that door.

FIONA: Rob, are you alright?

ROB: No, I am not. I'm stuck in here with a madman. They're all bloody mad.

NEIL: Stand back Rob, I'm coming through.

ROB: No! Get hold of him Fiona, don't let him touch that door. Don't let him do anything.

GLEN: Calm down Councillor, just tell them.

TERRY: And keep still.

ROB: Fiona, Neil, I want you to listen very carefully.

NEIL: There's no point, mun.

ROB: There's a very good point if you just bloody listen! Alright? Now this Terry bloke has a gun pointed at my — well, he has a gun pointed at me. Now this is the bloke who did the wine bar so he's mad enough to do anything. So I think we should let them do what they want. Show the film, whatever they want. So can you go and tell them please? (*Silence.*) Let them do what they want. (*Silence.*) OK?

FIONA: I can't. They've all gone. It's over.

ROB: What do you mean it's over, how can it be over? I'm still here.

FIONA: But no-one else is. It's just us.

ROB: What?

NEIL: Aye, they've pissed off, Rob.

ROB: They can't have.

TERRY: He's bluffing.

GLEN: He doesn't know how to.

EDDIE: Have you fixed the lights?

NEIL: Have we shit. Some bright spark's buggered 'em good and proper.

EDDIE: Brilliant. Told you, didn't I?

SAL: What we going to do, Glen?

TERRY: Ace card here, we do what we like.

EDDIE: Looks like a dead hand, Terry. If they've gone.

TERRY: Says them.

ROB: They've got it wrong, they must have.

GLEN: Let's see, shall we?

TERRY: No way. They could have anyone out there.

GLEN: Open it, Eddie.

           (*EDDIE goes to the door.*)

TERRY: You're chucking it away, chucking it all away.

           (*door opens*)

EDDIE: Just the two of them.

NEIL: Right, headcase, put that thing down now. I'm warning you, Terry. Glen, tell him.

ROB: Will someone tell me what's going on?

FIONA: I think you should put it down, Terry. It's over. They've all gone. Just packed up and went. Switched over to somewhere else. They didn't think this was worth it.

ROB: Not worth it! (*points madly at the gun*) This is not a water pistol pointed at my bollocks.

           (*Terry tosses the gun on the floor.*)

TERRY: It may as well be.

ROB: I don't believe this. A leading councillor abducted and threatened with violence and you're telling me everyone's disappeared. How? Why?

NEIL: Well, it's something I said, I suppose. Didn't think they'd go. Just thought they'd carry on. Without you like. It's the old man's fault. He said it first. Something your father said. But I got you out though, Rob. Stopped their game. That's what matters, innit?

GLEN: Something my father said?

NEIL: Aye. Two soft boys and a couple of daft tarts.

SAL: Who they didn't think were serious.

GLEN: Just a prank.

SAL: And just a poxy little Councillor.

GLEN: Where is he?

FIONA: In the hall.

          (*She goes out.*)

NEIL: Eh, stay where you are. I want you lot in one place and him somewhere else. (*to* TERRY) You, don't move an inch. (*He sheepishly picks up the gun and goes after her.*)

ROB: This is not happening. They can't have left me, they can't.

SAL: Why not? You're with us, and they left us years ago. All us useless sods. You were supposed to sweep us up and brush us down. Ballsed it, haven't you? They think you're a useless sod now. Probably sorting out a museum for you this minute. A waxwork Council full of useless sods.

ROB: If they'd known what they, what he was threatening —

TERRY: They still wouldn't have given a toss. Nobody cares. They're uncaring bastards, you're an uncaring bastard and I'm an uncaring bastard. A useless, uncaring bastard.

EDDIE: Not useless, mun. You blow up wine bars.

FIONA: Fifteen minutes of fame.

TERRY: Nah, a five minute kick. That's all you got for us. Red rose, red wine and stuffed olives. Where's the meat in that? Where's the fucking life? (*She says nothing.*) Eh Eddie, make yourself useful, get the lights back on.

EDDIE: Right. See where we are. (*He goes.*)

TERRY: See, he can do that. What do you do? What the

hell do you do?

ROB: I do this. I do all this. Today. I'm responsible for it all. I'm responsible.

FIONA: We know exactly what we do.

TERRY: Yeah, you supply the olives. But you don't get to eat them. Eh Sal, we had a taste today, didn't we? I think it's time we showed 'em the meat, what you say?

(*cut to*)

(*SAL'S film on the screen. We see CLEM'S silhouette.*)

CLEM: They should have had Zorro up there. Saturday afternoon, Zorro. Or Batman, or Superman or some such super, clever bugger. Saturday night was different, proper films then. Should have had a proper film up there. Anything. Anything but —

GLEN: Anything but us.

CLEM: You butting in again?

GLEN: Thought I was joining you.

CLEM: My protest, right? My hall.

GLEN: Ours.

CLEM: Mine. My hall they're taking. My history they're hijacking.

GLEN: We're still here. Living it. We're more than a film.

CLEM: More than a book. Roy Orbison and all.

GLEN: All part of it. All part of us.

(*CLEM looks up at screen.*)

CLEM: Not just a strike we lost. Bastard voice.

GLEN: Got it back today.

CLEM: Aye, you bloody did. You big daft tart.

NEIL: Is that your speech?

GLEN: What's left of it.

NEIL: Lucky there's no bugger left to hear it then.

GLEN: Perhaps I'm speaking for myself. Perhaps I'm speaking for you.

NEIL: Oh great, I got a woman speaking for me now. Wonderful. Or perhaps it's the mad bastard with a gun speaking for me. Even better.

GLEN: Perhaps.

NEIL: Hear that, Clem? Soft boys and daft tarts speaking for us now. How about that?

CLEM: Who does speak for you, Neil?

NEIL: I speak for myself, right.

CLEM: And what do you say?

NEIL: I say, I say we stop pissing about and get on with it. I say we help Rob and Fiona get back on their feet. Give 'em a bit of support. Me and you Glen, we can be up there with them. Get back to where we were. Please Glen, there's a place, I know there is.

GLEN: As a security guard.

NEIL: We've got parts to play in this. It's a new world. Rebirth. Regeneration.

CLEM: Heard it before, Neil. It's not you.

NEIL: It is. It's what I want.

(The film stops on one image. Two men and two women laughing, their arms around one another.)

GLEN: Soft boys and daft tarts. Remember, Neil? Remember. Remember for yourself, remember for me. Please.

NEIL: It's just a film. History.

GLEN: Ours. Our history. Our dream. We all got one. Lost and found. Even my mad brother with a gun. Found his. Showed us. His way. Mad bastard. Mad lost bastard. Lost and found. (*NEIL goes to leave. She shouts after him.*) Dreams.

(*Same image remains on the screen. Two men and two women, laughing. Roy Orbison 'In Dreams'.*)

End

Cradle To The Grave

Cradle to the Grave was first performed on Wed, Feb 5th, 1997 by third year students at the Welsh College of Music and Drama in the Bute Theatre, WCMD, Cardiff. Made in Wales commissioned the piece.

CHARACTERS

QUILLER	Paul Maddaford
DEREK	Robert Dugay
DR LEE	Trudy Tennent
BEVAN	David Maybrick
MARIE	Lise Mahoney
LAURA	Wendy Albiston
JOE	Richard Lynson
GILLESPIE	Richard Lomas
DAD	Oliver Ryan
CAROL	Nicola Westmoore
RUTH	Aimee Thomas
FEELGOOD/	
MENDLESON	Tom Pike
ANIMAL/DOCTOR	Andrew Sterry
CHRISTIAN/NURSE	Anthony Topham
Director	Jeff Teare
Asst. Director	Rebecca Gould
Design Supervisor	Sean Crowley
Costume Supervisor	Libby Hart
Production	Neil Marcus
Set Design	Gerwyn Lloyd
Assistants	Crispin Lowrey
	Nicola Thorpe
Costume Design	Lisa Clunis
Assistant	Sheryl Owens

STAGE MANAGEMENT

SM	Jo Nield
DSM	Emma Mitchell
ASM	Sally McElhayer
LX Design	Jim Mayer
Board Operator	Laura Sands
Sound Design	Roshan Patel
Technical Assist.	1st Year Group

Act One

(A central area is ringed by five dim pools of light. A night light, a burning cigarette, a harsh strip light, a soft bedside lamp, and the blue glow of a PC. The nightlight grows until we can see a figure asleep in an armchair. He is covered in a blanket so we can barely make him out but we clearly hear the rattle of his breath. Alongside him is a young man, QUILLER, who is holding some flowers.)

QUILLER: Flowers at midnight. They always smell sweeter. That's what you said Dad, wannit?

(The strip light snaps full on cued by a loud scream. We see a woman, MARIE, on a bed flanked by two midwives, RUTH and CAROL.)

MARIE: For Christ's sake, how much longer?

RUTH: Nearly there now, Marie.

MARIE: Where is the little bastard?

CAROL: We'll be seeing baby's head soon.

MARIE: I mean my husband, I'm talking about my sodding husband.

RUTH: I'm sure he'll be coming soon.

MARIE: That's his problem, he's always coming too bloody soon, that's why I'm here. And where's the doctor? I want a bloody doctor.

CAROL: You're doing fine Marie, you won't be needing a doctor, I assure you.

MARIE: No, but my husband will when I batter the

145

bastard. It's because I told him it's not his, that's why he's not here. 'Course it's his. Only something belonging to him could be this awkward. (*screams again*) Jesus Christ, where the hell is he?

RUTH: (*to each other*) Doctor Lee is on call, isn't she?

CAROL: Yes, but she doesn't seem to be answering her bleeper.

RUTH: Abandoned ship like the rest of them. And I thought it was women and children first.

(*QUILLER'S FATHER sits up.*)

DAD: Who smells flowers at midnight?

QUILLER: (*looks at the figure*) Who sells flowers at midnight? You would. That's what you said Dad, wannit? Get down to the Labour Ward at midnight, you'll clean up. Say it with flowers. Get well soon, we won't forget you, be h-a-p-p-y. Flowers for all occasions. Births, deaths, and all points in between. From the cradle...

(*He stops, takes the time to look around at the lights, listens, looks back to the nightlight.*)

QUILLER: ...to all bits in between. Maternity at midnight, that's where you should be, Dad. Selling flowers at midnight.

DAD: Who sells flowers at midnight?

(*QUILLER looks at the flowers, looks away. There is the sound of a buzzer, the lights come up on the cigarette. We see a young woman. She is smoking and drinking from a medical beaker. She looks at the buzzer.*)

DR. LEE: Fucky offski to you, fucky offski to you, fucky offski Doctor Lee, fucky offski to you. Happy birthday to me. (*She drinks. The buzzer goes off again*.) And there's only one of me. (*She drops it into the beaker*.)

(*Back to the nightlight. QUILLER'S FATHER drifts in and out of sleep.*)

QUILLER: Did Grandad sell flowers when you were born there? And when you had your tonsils out? And when I had those fourteen beads removed that I stuck up my nose? You said I could have died. You said I would have if it hadn't have been for Nye Bevan. I used to think it was him who got the beads down. You said it was him who paid for the medicine that killed the infection. Tell us about the start, Dad. Forty-eight. You were the first, weren't you? First on the steps. Cardiff City Peoples'. Nye's foundation stone. You were first on the payroll. Well flowersellers weren't on the payroll but Bevan bought flowers off you, didn't he? So you were the first. You always said flowers should be on the NHS. All part of the service. What did Bevan look like? Didn't have a bollard on his head, did he? He looks big. Big in that statue. Big man, wasn't he?

DAD: Memorial. Bloody memorial stone.

QUILLER: What?

DAD: Fourteen beads up your nose. Saved your life. (*He drifts away.*)

(*The bedside lamp gains focus. A man in bed, thirtysomething, NYE LLOYD BEVAN. He has a tray of food, wineglass in hand, bottle resting in ice bucket.*)

BEVAN: If there is more coffee, nurse. When you're ready. And please, no more Mister Bevan. It's Lloyd. Ignore what's written down. Most people can't even spell it let alone — It was my father's idea of a little joke. Something to remember him by. No one's remembered me, have they? Flowers would have been nice. Small gesture of remembrance. Or at least a card. One measly card Frances, that wouldn't have killed you. My wife, Frances. Well I say my wife, it's only by marriage. It's not by blood, or love or anything like that. But after five years it's the very best she could have done. It's down to her I'm in this position after all. Five years of stress and trauma enough to break any man's heart let alone — (*He nervously strokes his chest, looks at the wine.*) Perhaps it should have been red. Earthy, Latin diet and all that. Still I'm sure the boeuf en daube a la nicoise did the trick. I can positively feel its oily fingers massaging the old cardo-vasculars this very minute. (*strokes his chest rather more robustly*) I'll be right as rain in the morning. That cab is booked for ten, isn't it? Perhaps I'll get a run in before the meeting. Charge myself up. Give the adrenalin a pump. (*touches his chest more gingerly*) Perhaps not. Oh Jesus Christ, why can't someone else do it. (*He takes a drink... he immediately shows some discomfort and alarm.*) Nurse, nurse. (*presses buzzer*) Nurse.

(*more labour screams*)

RUTH: Could you try Doctor again, I think we might want a bit of needlework?

CAROL: Perhaps she's busy.

RUTH: Yes, she's a doctor isn't she? We're only midwives.

(*DR LEE pours herself another drink to the sound of her buzzer.*)

DR. LEE: (*singing*) One Dr Lee, there's only one Dr Lee, one Dr Lee-ee, there's only one Dr Lee. Morphine and tonic. The perfect birthday cocktail. You don't forget how old you are, you just forget who you are.

(*She slugs it back and slumps a little more.*)

(*QUILLER'S FATHER shows some distress.*)

QUILLER: Mam will be here soon. And the nurse'll be here tomorrow. It's only a dream, Dad. Bad dream. Nightmare. What the hell you doing here, Dad? Like this. They made a promise. You said they promised. No room at the inn. It's not the Marriot, it's supposed to be hospital. Pay as you die. Well you're not dying Dad, and you've already paid. We all have. You got a right to be in there. Foundation stone. Our foundation stone.

(*another scream from the Labour Ward*)

RUTH: You're making history here. The last baby to have the last word.

MARIE: And it'll be the last shag for that husband as well.

(*Focus returns to the nightlight.*)

QUILLER: I'll leave the light. You like a light. Mam will be in soon. Last one out turn the lights off. That's what they say, isn't it? (*He looks out at the lights.*)

DAD: Foundation stone, that's what he said. I told him... (*drifts away*)

QUILLER: What? What did you tell him, Dad?

DAD: Fourteen beads. How the hell do you get fourteen beads up your nose?

QUILLER: You were the first, Dad. Born there, first on the steps, the flower seller. Mister Bevan bought flowers off you. Part of the service. From the cradle.... They promised, they can't just shut you out. Close us down. Mister Bevan wouldn't. And I won't either. I'm the flower seller now. And no one's turning any lights off. We'll give them flowers at midnight, you'll see. You, me and Mister Bevan. They want a memorial, we'll give him one. (*He goes out.*)

(*The glow of the PC increases. A thirtysomething woman, LAURA, is gazing out of the window. A young man, GILLESPIE, is working on the PC.*)

GILLESPIE: Twenty five percent private intake.

LAURA: Good.

GILLESPIE: Target. Thirty percent in twelve months.

LAURA: Good. Good to look back at where you've been.

GILLESPIE: Is there anything else?

LAURA: That's why I chose this wing.

GILLESPIE: If there isn't —

LAURA: So I could always see that Victorian nightmare.

GILLESPIE: I do have a sort of a date.

LAURA: One light left. What is that? Is it the morgue?

GILLESPIE: No. Morgues don't have windows. It's Maternity. That's the last ward.

LAURA: Shame. I was hoping the last word would be a death. If you see what I mean.

GILLESPIE: I said ward. Not word. Last ward.

LAURA: What?

GILLESPIE: Nothing. Is there anything else?

LAURA: I've got this dull ache in my back. Kidneys I think.

GILLESPIE: It's just that I've got this —

LAURA: Look up renal for me.

GILLESPIE: Renal. (*He types in "renal".*)

LAURA: Artery, bi-pass, failure. No, I don't think so.

GILLESPIE: Perhaps you should see a doctor.

LAURA: I try not to see doctors, Gillespie. Not if I can help it.

GILLESPIE: Just as well you're running a hospital then.

LAURA: You say some very peculiar things sometimes. I do wish that light would go out. It's like waiting for the credits to end.

(*We hear 'Everything Must Go'* — *The Manic Street Preachers. QUILLER enters the central area wearing a walkman and pushing a flower trolley. Overhead we see a sign, CARDIFF CITY PEOPLES' HOSPITAL. He pushes the trolley up to a multi-directional sign: Casualty, X-ray, Physiotherapy, Maternity, etc, stares at it for a while, takes off the walkman. Music stops.*)

QUILLER: It's good they give you a choice. Everything you want there. Everything the sick man could ask for. Except you don't, do you? Have a choice. Not once you got this far. You can hardly say I fancy a bit of radiotherapy today or a go on the old physio bench. 'Cos once you're here your card is marked. Shame. But if you did have a choice, and I do, well I did, well I'd go for Maternity every time. Fags and alcohol for the labour and for the apres-birth, well by then they're dull enough to buy a bunch of poison ivy. Now casualty, that's a no go zone, they won't buy a sprig of bastard heather down there. It's all by appointment now. Casualty by appointment. What they on? I'd like to book in for Friday week, I got a feeling I'm going to fall on a pointed stick. When there was a casualty.

(*Two nurses come on. One takes away the sign.*)

Everything must go.

NURSE: Last one out, Quiller.

QUILLER: Not yet. (*gestures towards Maternity*)

NURSE: Still a bit late for that.

QUILLER: Never too late for flowers.

NURSE: You sound like your father.

QUILLER: 'Course I do. I'm the flower seller now.

NURSE: Yeah. How is he?

QUILLER: Great. Smelling flowers at midnight.

NURSE: Perhaps they'll move him to the 'New' now.

QUILLER: They don't want the old at the 'New'.

NURSE: Well, I'll see you there anyway.

QUILLER: Don't want me neither. They got a supermarket.

NURSE 2: Tell me about it, I'm probably on the checkout.

(*A young man, JOE, rushes on.*)

JOE: I'm looking for Maternity.

QUILLER: You're looking for eternity?

JOE: Maternity, Maternity.

QUILLER: Your wife's having a baby, isn't she?

JOE: What do you know about it?

QUILLER: I'm the man you're looking for.

JOE: She is lying. That is my baby, I don't care what she says.

QUILLER: Good. So you'll be wanting flowers.

152

JOE: I do not want flowers. I just want some directions.

QUILLER: See those lights over there? That's the new hospital.

JOE: I know. I've just been there. They told me she was still here.

QUILLER: Best place for her.

JOE: But there's bugger all here.

QUILLER: Everything must go, see.

JOE: Look, this is still a hospital?

QUILLER: Ghost hospital.

JOE: Can you just tell me where Maternity is?

QUILLER: Follow the light.

JOE: Follow the light.

QUILLER: Like in the Bible.

JOE: Listen, I am not looking for three shepherds and a donkey. I am looking for my wife.

QUILLER: Follow the light then. There's nothing else to follow. Except me.

JOE: What the hell are you doing selling flowers at this time, anyway?

QUILLER: I'm not selling 'em. They're free. On prescription. You could be the first.

JOE: Are you some sort of nutter? Or this is a bloody nightmare? (*He follows the light.*)

QUILLER: Could be. What do you say, Mister Bevan?

            (*QUILLER follows JOE with the trolley.*)

            (*A bedside lamp. A doctor is with Bevan.*)

BEVAN: Tell me I'm not dying, please tell me I'm not dying.

DOCTOR: You're not dying but we will have to transfer you.

BEVAN: You can't. I've paid for this bed.

DOCTOR: There is no Cardiac Unit here, Mr Bevan.

BEVAN: What the hell am I paying for then?

DOCTOR: Preferential treatment?

BEVAN: I'm certainly not paying for that sort of... (*stops short with real pain*) I can't breathe, doctor, I can't breathe.

DOCTOR: Just try and relax. We're just checking what beds are available.

BEVAN: I'm dreaming, I must be dreaming.

DOCTOR: Interesting diagnosis, Mr Bevan, but I think we'll take a raincheck on that one.

BEVAN: I musn't bugger up tomorrow, I musn't.

DOCTOR: Let's look after today, shall we?

(*DR LEE'S buzzer goes off.*)

DR. LEE: One Dr Lee. You think there's only one Dr Lee. Well there's not. There's lots of us now. Lots of Dr Lees to go round. The rounds. And round and round and round. One can go to Maternity and go stitch, stitch, stitch. And one can go to Casualty and go stitch, stitch, stitch, and one can do the wards and go stick, stitch, needle, stick. And then you can all come back to this beautiful... (*looks around*) Morgue. You can all come back to this beautiful Morgue and stitch my little head back on, stitch my little mouth up, stitch my ears up and stitch my little eyes up, so I can never, ever, never, ever, never — Where the hell are you, you bastard? (*She passes out.*)

(*Light on the PC. We see LAURA drinking a bottle of mineral water.*)

LAURA: This isn't carbonated. It has to be carbonated for the kidneys, surely.

GILLESPIE: That's all they had. Can I go now?

LAURA: I just want to see that light go out.

GILLESPIE: Well perhaps I can go over and switch it off.

LAURA: Nobody's going back there, Gillespie. Not unless they're driving a bulldozer anyway. It's nearly midnight, for god's sake. What sort of system allows babies to come out whenever they want to?

GILLESPIE: Perhaps you could replace it with an appointment system.

LAURA: I sometimes think you're in the wrong business, Gillespie. (*looks out of the window*) I don't know what the salvage firm are gong to say when they turn up and find a woman with her legs in the air. And I don't want your opinion on that, Gillespie.

GILLESPIE: Can't imagine there's anything left to salvage.

LAURA: I've talked up some very marketable assets over there. So the last thing they want to find is — well, it doesn't bear thinking about, does it?

GILLESPIE: No.

(*groans from Maternity*)

RUTH: That's lovely Marie, that's absolutely lovely.

MARIE: Please let it be a girl, please let it be a girl.

(*The baby is delivered.*)

RUTH: That's it, that's it, that's absolutely wonderful.

JOE: It's a boy. It's a boy.

RUTH: A beautiful baby girl.

MARIE: Let me see her, let me see her.

RUTH: You must be the father.

MARIE: Like hell.

RUTH: Better late than never.

MARIE: I wouldn't say that.

JOE: We've got a baby girl. A beautiful baby girl.

MARIE: I've got a baby girl Joe, you've just a stupid look
          on your face. Oh, let me hold her, let me hold her,
          let me hold my little baby. Hello baby, hello my
          baby. Where've you been all this time? Mammy's
          had such a hard time.

JOE: I'm really sorry I'm late.

MARIE: There's no point in just being around for the good
          bits, you know.

JOE: What good bits?

MARIE: Oh, piss off.

RUTH: I don't think this is a time for arguing.

JOE: No. It's not.

MARIE: What is it the time for then?

QUILLER: Flowers. That's what my father said. And his
          father. That's why we're here. (*He gives her a bunch
          of flowers.*)

RUTH: Quiller —

MARIE: They're beautiful.

CAROL: Quiller, what are you doing here?

QUILLER: My job.

MARIE: Who are they from?

QUILLER: Mister Bevan. All part of the service.

JOE: What Mr Bevan? What bloody service?

QUILLER: Those are very sad questions.

JOE: You are a very sad man.

MARIE: He is a very beautiful man.

JOE: Is this him? Is this the bastard? Or is it this Bevan bloke?

RUTH: Mr Bevan was capable of many things, but not posthumous conception.

JOE: What?

RUTH: No sign of Dr Lee?

CAROL: Not a bleep. I think it's her birthday.

RUTH: Oh well, it's down scalpels and head for the bar. I'll just have to do it myself. You look after baby. (*hands BABY to CAROL*) You look after the flowers. (*hands flowers to JOE*) And I'll look after mum.

QUILLER: Do you want a hand?

RUTH: Quiller, you're the flower seller.

QUILLER: It's not the same, is it? People never used to argue up here. It used to be beautiful. The best place. My father loved it.

RUTH: Your father was making money.

QUILLER: My father was earning money. Same as you.

RUTH: Sorry, Quiller. I know he was. I didn't mean that. It's been a long night. If you want to give a hand why don't you try and keep security out of Maternity.

QUILLER: Keep security out of Maternity?

RUTH: Quiller, some things you must not even begin to think about. Like why are you here and why are you giving away flowers? (*She stops.*) No. No.

Definitely no. I do not want to know the answer. (*She gets on with her work.*)

(*QUILLER and JOE are out the front.*)

JOE: I'm not paying for them.

QUILLER: That's true.

JOE: Are you alright?

QUILLER: I've been better.

JOE: I don't feel too brilliant. In fact I feel like shit.

QUILLER: You're in the right place.

JOE: Maternity?

QUILLER: Hospital.

JOE: This is not a hospital.

QUILLER: Just hasn't got the sign, that's all. I saw our librarian in the swimming baths once. She had her hair tied back and was wearing a black Speedo one-piece. She hit the pool without a sound and then cut the water like a blade. I didn't recognise her. Then I remembered and swam past and asked her if *Day Of The Jackal* had been returned. She was still a librarian, see?

JOE: You are a nutter.

QUILLER: That's your baby in there.

JOE: I know it is. I don't care what she says.

QUILLER: Pretty soon your wife's going to come out. She'll give you the baby all wrapped up in a warm, soft blanket, you'll give her the flowers, you'll walk to the car and two smiling nurses will wave you off from the steps. This is a good place.

(*JOE looks back in, then out front, then at QUILLER.*)

JOE: I'll look forward to that.

QUILLER: And me.

(Sound of ambulance. Paramedic, DEREK, pushes wheelchair towards Maternity. In the wheelchair is BEVAN wrapped in a blanket and wearing an oxygen mask.)

JOE: Bloody hell, I like his style, gas and air even before the wife arrives.

DEREK: What's happened to Accident and Emergency?

QUILLER: Closed up this afternoon.

DEREK: Where've they put reception?

QUILLER: Closed this morning.

DEREK: Well, I want the Cardiac Unit.

QUILLER: Closed yesterday.

DEREK: Well, what's this?

QUILLER: Maternity. Closing any minute.

JOE: Yeah. I've just had a baby.

DEREK: Congratulations, but this man is having a heart attack, now can you let me through, please?

JOE: There's only midwives in there. I don't think they do heart attacks.

DEREK: This is an emergency.

JOE: *(blocking his way)* And that is my wife.

DEREK: I'm not interested in your wife.

(CAROL comes out.)

CAROL: What is going on?

DEREK: Patient with suspected cardiac arrest. Transfer from Cyncoed Court Hospital.

CAROL: That's a private hospital.

DEREK: Yeah, so it's probably only indigestion, I know. But there he is.

CAROL: Well, he can't stay here. This is Maternity and nothing else. We don't even have a doctor. Well, we do. Somewhere.

DEREK: Well you better find him before his indigestion gets serious.

CAROL: We can't help him. There's nothing here. We're closing. The hospital is closing. It's a dead hospital.

DEREK: Well, it's going to have a dead patient. Because I am transferring — (*he reads from papers*) Aneurin Bevan from Cyncoed Court to Cardiac Unit Cardiff City Peoples' Hospital.

QUILLER: Aneurin Bevan?

CAROL: Well, it's a mistake.

QUILLER: It's a miracle.

DEREK: It was in the computer. Black and white. Aneurin Bevan transfer to —

(*QUILLER snatches the papers from him.*)

QUILLER: Aneurin Lloyd Bevan.

CAROL: It's impossible, you can't transfer him here, the whole hospital's been transferred. There's nothing here.

DEREK: Well, there must be. The computer's located a spare bed here.

CAROL: Of course there's a spare bed here, there's four hundred spare beds here. But I bet your computer can't locate a single spare doctor, or a spare nurse or a spare flaming toilet cleaner. We're shut.

DEREK: All I know —

QUILLER: (*holding the paper in front of an increasingly worked*

160

up BEVAN) You're Aneurin Bevan? Nye Bevan?

DEREK: I shouldn't mention that to him. Seems to get him agitated.

CAROL: Look, you'll have to take him over to the New.

DEREK: I'm just contracted to bring him here.

CAROL: Well, you can't.

DEREK: I've got other emergencies to deal with, you know.

CAROL: Are these private emergencies? Is there an epidemic of indigestion in Cyncoed at the moment?

DEREK: I just do what they pay me to do.

CAROL: Leaving patients on the steps.

DEREK: You are leaving patients on the steps.

CAROL: Well, there's no point in taking him into the Labour Ward.

DEREK: So you're going to leave him on the steps?

(They all look at BEVAN.)

JOE: There you are mate, you're alright, no one's going to leave you on the steps. Well, actually someone is, but no, no one's going to own up to it. Unless it's you. Yes, it's the flower seller, the flower seller is going to leave a patient on the steps. What an irresponsible bastard.

QUILLER: You can't leave Nye Bevan on the steps.

(BEVAN rips the mask off.)

BEVAN: It's Lloyd, it's bloody Lloyd, alright, and I'm having a heart attack and I'm paying a lot of money for it and I don't have a lot of time.

DEREK: There you are, if you won't listen to me, listen to the patient.

CAROL: Get him in quickly.

QUILLER: Lloyd?

(*They push him in.*)

JOE: Give him an epidural, he'll be alright.

QUILLER: (*reading the papers again*) It's his middle name, that's what it is. Lloyd's his middle name.

(*RUTH is just finishing with MARIE.*)

RUTH: There, just one tiny stitch. I don't know what it is with doctors. They spend seven years training and all they want to do is practice their needlework. It's the men, really. I think they see childbirth as an excuse to stitch women up. They'd look at it differently if they had babies themselves.

(*She turns around to see BEVAN and co.*)

RUTH: I'm sorry. It was a joke. An hypothesis. Men do not have babies.

JOE: It's his heart.

RUTH: I'm a midwife. What do you want me to do, deliver it?

CAROL: They've sent him here from Cyncoed Court.

RUTH: That's private medicine for you, have a heart attack, end up in Maternity.

DEREK: Look, it was the computer —

CAROL: Who told him to bring him here?

DEREK: I have a contract —

CAROL: Which says he can't take him away.

DEREK: Look, I have another emergency —

RUTH: Computer virus?

DEREK: The computer said you had a free bed.

162

RUTH: Trouble with computers is they don't read the right papers. Now Mr —

RUTH: (*reading*) Aneurin Lloyd Bevan.

BEVAN: (*ripping the mask off again*) Are you deliberately trying to kill me off? Is that it? Is that the NHS today? National bloody homicide.

RUTH: I think you should calm down, Aneurin —

BEVAN: It's Lloyd, right? Lloyd, Mister Bevan or nothing at all. (*rams the mask back on*)

RUTH: Not quite at death's door yet then. Keep your finger on that buzzer, she's bound to be somewhere. We'll have a doctor with you in a moment, Lloyd.

QUILLER: That's just his middle name.

RUTH: No Quiller, that's his name. Now take him through to the ante-room and call me if he shows any signs of distress. But he won't. Will he? (*QUILLER shakes his head.*) Now strange as this may seem, I have a mother and baby to deal with. And possibly a father.

DEREK: Look, I don't mean to go on about contracts —

RUTH: Well, don't. You are a paramedic, I am a midwife, he is a flower seller. Now in terms of medical care that sounds like a contract made in hell, but somewhere between us I think we can contrive to keep this poor sod alive for the next five minutes.

(*BEVAN slowly takes the mask off to speak. He can't.*)

CAROL: When she says five minutes she actually means —

RUTH: Until the doctor gets here. I'm sure someone will eventually remember we're still here.

MARIE: Does anyone remember I'm still here?

RUTH: Joseph, time to meet your wife. And your

beautiful baby daughter.

(*JOE joins his wife.*)

QUILLER: You're in good hands, Mister Bevan. (*He pushes him off.*) All the arms of the NHS are here. Just for you.

(*He puts the mask back on. They wheel him to one side. Split focus on the three groups: Joe, Marie and baby, Quiller, Derek and Bevan, and the two midwives. The midwives are cleaning up, taking off gloves, overalls, etc.*)

RUTH: All arms of the NHS. Maternity and Morgue.

CAROL: The cradle and the grave.

RUTH: I'm sure there used to be something in between.

DEREK: I'm not responsible.

QUILLER: 'Course you're not.

DEREK: I am not responsible for this patient any more.

QUILLER: You've discharged your responsibility.

DEREK: I've got responsibilities elsewhere.

QUILLER: That you have to attend to.

JOE: I hate these places.

MARIE: Why didn't you say? We could have stayed at home and you could have done it yourself.

JOE: No, when I said I hate these places —

MARIE: You were just being thick.

JOE: Yeah.

DEREK: I've fulfilled my commitments.

QUILLER: 'Course you have.

DEREK: I've got other calls.

QUILLER: Emergencies.

DEREK: Non stop.

QUILLER: You're an ambulance driver.

DEREK: Paramedic.

QUILLER: You're needed.

DEREK: He needs a doctor.

QUILLER: There's one on the way.

MARIE: You should have been here, Joe.

JOE: Yeah, I should have been here.

MARIE: Your baby.

JOE: My baby?

MARIE: 'Course it's your baby. Who else takes that long coming?

JOE: But I thought you thought —

MARIE: I was having a baby. I'm allowed to think the worst of everyone. Especially you.

JOE: Yeah.

QUILLER: You can leave him with me.

DEREK: I can't leave a patient with you.

QUILLER: You were just going to leave him on the steps.

DEREK: You're just a flower seller.

QUILLER: Just? There's nothing just about me. There's nothing just about anyone. My grandfather was the flowerseller, my father was the flowerseller. He sold Nye Bevan flowers in nineteen forty-eight. The first National Health worker. Cardiff City Peoples' Hospital. If you can't trust me with a patient, who can you trust?

(*They look at BEVAN.*)

QUILLER: He needs rest.

DEREK: He's paid for it.

QUILLER: He don't have to. This is a free bed.

DEREK: He's their responsibility now.

QUILLER: He couldn't be in better hands.

DEREK: First bloke I've delivered to Maternity.

QUILLER: Go down in history. (*considers this, then goes*)

RUTH: Last baby to be delivered in Maternity.

CAROL: She'll be in the papers.

MARIE: I want to go home.

JOE: But you can't go home.

MARIE: But I want to go home.

JOE: Who'll look after you?

MARIE: You.

JOE: But this is a hospital.

MARIE: And you're a father.

JOE: Yeah. Right.

MARIE: My mother was born here. Stayed for a week. I stayed for three days. And this one, in and out. What what will I do with the next?

RUTH: Have it at home.

           (*They get up. They start to walk out. MARIE hands the baby to JOE. He hands the flowers to MARIE. The midwives help them.*)

MARIE: Shall we go home?

JOE: Yeah, the car's this — (*He stops, looks back, the midwives wave. QUILLER is pushing the bed out of sight.*)

MARIE: What's wrong?

166

JOE: Nothing. That bloke, the flower seller. I didn't pay him. For the flowers.

MARE: He gave them to us.

(They walk towards the car.)

CAROL: Wonder what they'll call her.

RUTH: Aneurin Bevan.

CAROL: What?

RUTH: Aneurin Bevan. He's having a heart attack in the ante room.

(They turn. Lights up on the PC.)

LAURA: Excruciating pain behind my left eye now.

GILLESPIE: You know what that is, don't you?

LAURA: Yes, I do know what that is, thank you.

GILLESPIE: It's stress.

LAURA: And it is not stress.

GILLESPIE: Just forget it then. Go home and forget it.

LAURA: Forget it? Hospital administration is not about forgetting it. I have a security firm employed from midnight, a salvage company engaged at nine, a property developer arriving at twelve and in the middle of this I have a woman having a baby. What sort of hospital administration does that look like?

GILLESPIE: When you put it like that —

LAURA: Can you look up neuralgia. Neural -gia. OK?

(The two midwives. No sign of QUILLER.)

CAROL: Perhaps it was a dream.

RUTH: A nightmare.

CAROL: A joke.

RUTH: Heard the one about the paramedic, a flower seller and Nye Bevan?

CAROL: Not to mention the vanishing house doctor.

RUTH: Well, they've all buggered off somewhere.

CAROL: Dr Lee's birthday party?

RUTH: Or Mr Bevan's funeral.

CAROL: Don't. What was Quiller doing here, anyway?

RUTH: Following his father's footsteps.

CAROL: Haunting Maternity?

RUTH: Selling flowers at midnight. Poor soul.

CAROL: Is he dead now?

RUTH: As good as. Left for dead you could say. Too old to spend money on.

            (*They both look around.*)

CAROL: But he's not being replaced.

RUTH: You couldn't. He was called Quiller too. He was first in here when it became National Health. Sold Nye Bevan flowers apparently. Right on these steps.

            (*They look back in, then at each other.*)

RUTH: Carol, some things you must not even begin to think about.

CAROL: No. I wasn't going to.

RUTH: Right. Last one out, turn the lights off. Whoever you are.

            (*They leave. The lights go out.*)

(*LAURA at the window. GILLESPIE asleep at the PC.*)

LAURA: Alleluia.

GILLESPIE: What? Sorry. Neuralgia, the er... paroxysmal intermittent pain along the course of a nerve.

LAURA: It's over.

GILLESPIE: Oh good, that's a relief for you — oh sorry — congratulations, what did you have, boy or a girl?

LAURA: That Gillespie, that light going out, is the final closing of a door, the last page in a chapter —

GILLESPIE: The final nail in the coffin.

LAURA: The dark before a new dawn, Gillespie.

GILLESPIE: So what's it going to be anyway? After they've salvaged the life out of it.

LAURA: Well, I'm meeting representatives of Macdonald's tomorrow.

GILLESPIE: I thought they'd moved in here.

LAURA: This is a hospital.

GILLESPIE: With a Macdonalds.

LAURA: Well, yes.

GILLESPIE: And an Interflora.

LAURA: Yes.

GILLESPIE: In fact, it's the biggest shopping mall outside St David's Centre.

LAURA: Hospitals have to change. Reacting to the market and serving the client.

GILLESPIE: Lots of people liked that hospital.

LAURA: A lot of people like outside toilets but I for one have no intention of sitting in the cold and rain wiping my bottom with the *Daily Mirror*.

GILLESPIE: No, I can't see you doing that.

LAURA: Why are you still here, anyway?

GILLESPIE: What — why am I — oh, I thought I'd hang around for the celebrations.

LAURA: Celebrations? (*looks out of the window*) Well there's certainly cause, Gillespie. There's certainly cause.

GILLESPIE: (*following her gaze*) What do you think they had in the end? Boy or a girl?

LAURA: See you in the morning, Gillespie.

(*He goes. She winces and rubs her temple. Goes to the PC.*)

(*The sound of 'Design for Life' by the Manic Street Preachers fills the space. We see QUILLER, headphones on, pushing BEVAN in a bed. He is asleep. The music subsides.*)

QUILLER: What you dreaming, Mister Bevan? Hope you're not dreaming this. 'Cos when you wake up, it'll still be true. Abandoned ship. Ghost ship now. Rats left first. Vermin. Remember them, Mister Bevan? They're across there now watching us sink. My father should be here. Remember my father? You bought flowers off him. He didn't jump ship, they pushed him, pushed him overboard, sink or swim. You saved my life, remember, those beads up my nose? Well, I know it wasn't you, but — (*stops, looks round*) quiet, innit? No doctors, nurses, no men pushing trolleys, no hot linen, cold tea, bags of blood, bottles of piss, men selling flowers. They're going to have men selling beefburgers, Mister Bevan. Men in stupid stripey shirts selling stupid stripey beefburgers. (*looks at BEVAN*) You need a doctor. This hospital needs a doctor. They were never on your side, were they? They are now Mister Bevan, you'll see. Mister Bevan? (*He is in a deep sleep.*) Don't worry Mister Bevan, I'll get you a doctor. And nurses. And food, yeah, we need food. Don't you go away, I'm going to get it sorted.

(*He disappears, leaving BEVAN alone. All light has gone, save the blue of the hospital safety lights. There is a silence suddenly broken by the buzzer. DR LEE sits bolt upright as does BEVAN and QUILLER'S FATHER.*)

DAD: You promised. Remember, you bloody promised.

BEVAN: Doctor. Nurse. Doctor.

DR. LEE: I'm there, I'm there, I'm there. (*switches off the bleeper*) I'm there. (*looks around*) Where the fuck am I?

(*QUILLER'S FATHER collapses back.*)

BEVAN: Nurse. Anyone. Bloody flower seller will do. (*He looks around. There are some flowers on the bed. He picks one up.*) Frances? (*He calls out.*) Frances. Frances. I'm so cold. It's bloody freezing in here. (*calls out*) It's bloody freezing in here. (*looks at the flowers again*) Oh Jesus Christ, don't let me die. I can't die. I can't bloody die, I'm in BUPA for god's sake. I haven't paid all this money just — (*he shouts out*) just to be left to die. (*suddenly looks at his watch*) For pity's sake, I have a meeting at twelve o'clock. Where the hell is everyone? What sort of place is this?

DR. LEE: It's the Morgue. I'm in the fucking Morgue. What am I doing — oh thank you God, thank you, thank you, thank you. (*She lies back.*) If only. (*She sits up, holds her head.*) Oh, that hurt. Feel as if my head has just been stitched — (*stops as if to remember*) stitch, stitch, stitch. What happened to my birthday? What happened to — what the hell am I doing in the Morgue? Rounds. Round and round the hospital round. In the Morgue? That

171

would save time. (*The bleeper goes. She stares at it. Talks to the bleeper.*) Because there's not enough time. And there's not enough of me. And there's too many of you. You have to understand that. You really do. I have to make you understand that. Otherwise, (*She gets up.*) otherwise, stitch, stitch, stitch. Now where the hell are you?

(*She goes out.*)

BEVAN: Does anyone work in the place? (*silence*) Does anyone know I'm here? (*silence*) Does anyone actually know who I am? I am Lloyd Aneurin — (*he catches hold of his chest*) Oh Jesus, Oh Jesus, Oh Jesus. Oh Jesus, I need a bloody doctor. I want a bloody doctor. I've paid for a bloody doctor. Even if you're just going to stand and watch me die, I want a doctor. Or a nurse. Flower seller. Priest. Frances.

(*He passes out.*)

(*We hear 'Everything Must Go' — The Manics. Two people appear, CHRISTIAN and ANIMAL, dressed in overalls, industrial masks and hard hats. One is wielding a power saw, the other a power drill. One is carrying a ghetto blaster.*)

CHRISTIAN: Where do we start?

ANIMAL: Anywhere.

CHRISTIAN: What do we do?

ANIMAL: Take it out.

CHRISTIAN: Take what out?

ANIMAL: Everything.

CHRISTIAN: Everything?

ANIMAL: Trust me.

172

CHRISTIAN: I trust you.

ANIMAL: Everything must go.

CHRISTIAN: Everything must go.

> (*They start the machines up.*)

ANIMAL: (*starts to sing*) "And if you need an explanation, then everything must go...."

CHRISTIAN: (*joining in*) "And I just hope that you can forgive us, but everything must go...."

> (*They advance – a sharp-suited man walks in – MENDLESON – he watches them.*)

MEN.: Having fun?

> (*They see him and switch off.*)

ANIMAL: Mister Mendleson.

MEN.: What is this all about?

ANIMAL: It's a song.

CHRISTIAN: Nihilistic denial of post modernism.

ANIMAL: No it's not.

MEN: I am not talking about – (*he stops himself*) What were your instructions?

ANIMAL: Rip it out.

CHRISTIAN: Everything must go.

MEN.: Everything must – you're new to us, aren't you? Well your colleague here, Mr –

ANIMAL: Animal.

MEN.: Animal has been here for over six – I refuse to call you Animal. I refuse to believe that anyone would want to call you Animal.

ANIMAL: It's after that drummer in The Muppets.

CHRISTIAN: You play the drums?

ANIMAL: No.

MEN.:   I don't want to know any more. And if you tell me your name is Kermit because you look nothing like a frog —

CHRISTIAN: Christian. My name's Christian.

MEN.:   Good. I can deal with that. That's the sort of name that rests easily on a salvage worker. That's salvage, Animal, note the extra consonant from the word that you're mistaking it for.

ANIMAL: Even drummers can spell, Mister Mendleson.

MEN.:   But you're not a — no, no, we'll leave that one there. Do you know what you're doing? Exactly.

ANIMAL: We're gutting the place.

MEN.:   Gutting. Gutting. This place that you're "gutting" is an architectural timepiece, a veritable gold-mine of Victorian artefacts. I do not want you "gutting" the bollocks out of it.

ANIMAL: I do know the difference between artefacts and bollocks, Mister Mendleson.

MEN.:   I don't think you know the difference between artefacts and artex.

ANIMAL: Yeah, I do. Artefact's got a whole bunch of different consonants in it.

MEN.:   Right. OK. Fine. We've had the comedy, now let's survey the damage, shall we? For a start, where've you put the sign?

CHRISTIAN: What sign?

MEN.:   Cardiff City Peoples' Hospital? Some fine mid-century wrought iron work?

ANIMAL: There was no sign.

CHRISTIAN: We weren't sure we were in the right place.

MEN.: God help us. It's just as well Llandaff Cathedral is signposted, you'd have ended up gutting that.

ANIMAL: Perhaps someone nicked it.

MEN.: There's been round the clock security.

CHRISTIAN: Perhaps they nicked it.

ANIMAL: Or one of them nurses. As a memento.

MEN.: You think a nurse would actually — right, fine, let's leave that, shall we? Get down to some real work.

ANIMAL: Suits me, Mister Mendleson.

CHRISTIAN: Yeah, suits us.

MEN.: Right. We'll make a start in Maternity.

ANIMAL: What are going to find there?

CHRISTIAN: Edwardian afterbirth?

ANIMAL: Victorian foetus in a jar.

MEN.: I really have employed a pair of muppets, haven't I?

ANIMAL: No. (*silence, then he starts to sing*) "It's time to put on makeup, it's time to start the show...."

MEN.: In the Labour Ward surrounding what I believe they now call the Delivery Suite, there is some intricate and delicate friezework. I would like it taken down and removed with absolute care, love and attention. (*exits*)

ANIMAL: Love and attention.

CHRISTIAN: Care. Love and attention.

(*They start up the machines. They move towards the curtains around BEVAN'S bed. BEVAN comes to, screams.*)

ANIMAL: What the hell is he doing here?

175

CHRISTIAN: Having a baby?

ANIMAL: He shouldn't be here. He shouldn't be here, no way.

CHRISTIAN: Perhaps we shouldn't.

ANIMAL: Mister Mendleson! Mister Mendleson!

(*They leave.*)

(*LAURA at the computer. QUILLER comes in.*)

LAURA: Gillespie. I didn't expect you so early. How was your sort of date?

QUILLER: She didn't turn up.

LAURA: (*swinging around*) I'm sorry, I thought you were... I don't think you should be here.

QUILLER: I don't think you should be here.

LAURA: Well, I sometimes think that, but this is my office and I don't believe you have an appointment.

QUILLER: I don't believe I do. I don't believe a lot of things any more.

(*LAURA goes to pick up the telephone.*)

QUILLER: I don't want you to do that. You're supposed to be talking to me.

LAURA: What do you want?

QUILLER: I want a doctor.

LAURA: Well, you haven't really come to the right place.

QUILLER: Where do you suggest? The Post Office?

LAURA: If you require treatment then I suggest —

QUILLER: I form an orderly queue? Stretching several years. Unless of course I'm some useless old codger dying of cancer then I should join a much shorter queue outside the Morgue. No, I do not require any treatment, I require one doctor, possibly two, definitely two nurses and one porter. And a load of drugs.

LAURA: I think I should call someone, don't you?

QUILLER: You've got my order. And before you start messing it up, you should know that I've got Nye Bevan. Over there. In his hospital.

LAURA: In his — (*looks out the window*) That hospital is closed. Now I really think —

QUILLER: Then why has it got a patient in it then?

LAURA: A patient?

QUILLER: Who you should be looking after.

(*LAURA gets up and looks across to the hospital.*)

LAURA: Is this Mr Bevan, by any chance, having a baby?

QUILLER: No, he's having a heart attack. Over there. In his hospital. The Peoples' Hospital. Remember it?

LAURA: Yes, I do remember it. Very well. And I know that there is no one left in it. Not a soul. Or if there is they shouldn't be —

QUILLER: It's his hospital, 'course he should be there. Nye Bevan, his foundation, said so himself on those steps.

LAURA: Nye Bevan?

QUILLER: Yes. Heard of him?

LAURA: Yes, I believe I have.

QUILLER: Well, you'll know then, you'll know, won't you? You'll know all about it. He told my father. On those steps. Do you know my father?

LAURA: I'm sorry, I don't believe I do.

QUILLER: I'm sorry, I don't believe you do. Now he thinks it's a memorial. Our hospital. Probably because

177

	he's dying. His head's probably full of that stuff. Now if you don't give me a doctor and a nurse and drugs he's going to die anyway and I'll give him a memorial. Flowers at midnight. Right?
LAURA:	Right. Right, Mr —
QUILLER:	Quiller. But it's not Mr.
LAURA:	Right. I don't have to do this but I will. I will contact A and E for you. They will investigate. If they discover that it is a fraudulent call you will be charged for the callout and possibly prosecuted. Now, if you don't leave this office immediately, I will have you removed. (*picks up telephone*) Heart attack, you say?
QUILLER:	That's Nye Bevan, not my father.
LAURA:	Right. (*dials*) Hello, Chief Executive here — yes — well, I have an emergency for you — of sorts — possible incident at the City Hospital — yes I am aware that is closed — so let's call it an emergency transfer —

(*QUILLER cuts her off.*)

QUILLER:	No. No. Not a transfer. Nobody is being transferred. Not any more. I want doctors, nurses, porters, medication. The works. Over there. Where it belongs. Now. Please.
LAURA:	Now, I'd like you to listen to me very carefully. I will deal with your request, in my own way. But if you don't leave this office immediately, I will have to call the police and have you removed forcibly.
QUILLER:	You're not listening to me at all, are you? Now if you don't give me what I want, I will leave this office and I will give you what you want. What you all want. Understood?
LAURA:	Understood. (*she picks up the telephone*) I'm calling

the police.

(*QUILLER wrenches it out of it's socket.*)

LAURA: That wasn't very smart, was it?

QUILLER: I'm not very smart. I've very angry.

LAURA: You are in danger of doing something that you will regret.

QUILLER: Am I? Well, you'll have to advise me how to live with it then, 'cos you must be up to your neck in it.

LAURA: I think you should know, I want you to know, that I abhor violence.

QUILLER: Well I don't. I fucking hate it.

(*BEVAN, terrified, in his bed. MENDLESON, ANIMAL and CHRISTIAN return.*)

MEN.: Who the hell is he?

CHRISTIAN: Victorian artefact?

MEN.: What's he doing here? What the hell are you doing here?

BEVAN: What am I doing here? What are they doing here, you mean?

MEN.: They are doing whatever I tell them to do.

BEVAN: Well tell them to bugger off then. What sort of hospital is this?

MEN.: It is a hospital under my — can you turn those things off, please? (*They turn off the machines.*) Thank you. Perhaps we should start again. Can you tell me exactly what you're doing here?

BEVAN: I'm having a heart attack.

(*They look at one another.*)

ANIMAL: You don't want to have a heart attack here, this is Maternity.

MEN.:   Can you leave this to me, please?

BEVAN: What's he talking about?

MEN.:   He doesn't know what he's talking about.

BEVAN: I want to see a consultant.

MEN.:   Well, I suppose I am a sort of consultant.

BEVAN: What the hell is going on then?

MEN.:   Well, it is a fact, that we are indeed in Maternity. The Delivery Suite I believe.

BEVAN: Yes, of course it is and these two are about to perform a caesarian, I suppose?

MEN.:   You shouldn't be here.

BEVAN: I shouldn't be here. This is a Cardiac Unit. In a hospital. I am having a heart attack. Behind you are two masked men with chain saws and you tell me I shouldn't be here. Jesus Christ, this cannot be happening, this just cannot be happening.

MEN.:   Exactly who are you? Exactly.

BEVAN: I am exactly Aneurin Lloyd Bevan, that's who I am exactly. And I'm dying.

            (*They look at each other.*)

ANIMAL: That's that bloke in Queen Street with the bollard on his head.

CHRISTIAN: He was in the Merthyr riots.

ANIMAL: They hung him, didn't they? He was a shit hot dude.

MEN.:   He was the architect of the NHS, you pair of muppets. It's him that was responsible for all this lot.

(BEVAN finds the strength to grab hold of him.)

BEVAN: Look, I have been here a long time and I am dying. Do you understand that? I have been here a very long time and I have been left to die.

MEN.: I think you should let go, Mr Bevan.

BEVAN: *(right in his face)* It's Lloyd, right. Bloody Lloyd.

MEN.: Right, Mr — Lloyd. Exactly who left you to die?

BEVAN: *(shaking him loose)* You have. Your lot. The whole damn lot of you. *(collapses back)*

ANIMAL: They've forgotten him, haven't they? Dumped him, shut up shop and forgotten him.

CHRISTIAN: Poor bastard.

MEN.: You really shouldn't be here.

BEVAN: No, I shouldn't. I should be in Tuscany. Pasta, olives, char-grilled mullet. Frances pouring me a glass of Chianti. Jackie Kennedy on a motor bike, something smelling in the woodshed.... *(He drifts away.)*

ANIMAL: He's out of his head.

CHRISTIAN: Probably on drugs.

MEN.: Probably needs drugs.

ANIMAL: I can get him drugs. What do you reckon? Bit of whizz? That should get his ticker going.

MEN.: Can you be quiet. This is serious.

ANIMAL: Yeah, he needs an ambulance.

MEN.: Will you stop interrupting. Christian, I'd like you to call an ambulance. This is not on, this is really not on. I have a contract to gut this building.

CHRISTIAN: Salvage.

MEN.: What? Yes. Quite. And I am the contractor. And

what do I find?

ANIMAL: The architect.

MEN.: What?

ANIMAL: Of the NHS.

MEN.: Will you please be quiet. (*He takes out his mobile phone.*) I shall sort this out with Miss Chief Executive herself.

CHRISTIAN: Shouldn't we sort him out first?

MEN.: Right, right. (*hands him the phone*) You sort this out, I shall go and sort out Madam personally. Never know what we might find next. Tony Benn in the Psychiatric Ward. (*He waits for response to his 'joke'.*) Tony Benn. He's mad, isn't he? (*nothing*) Right. No one touches anything. Except for him. And only if they're wearing a uniform.

ANIMAL: Ambulance drivers don't wear uniforms no more.

CHRISTIAN: Yeah they do, they wear those green baggy numbers. Like combat suits. Dead cool.

MEN.: Thank you. Right. Action please.

(*He goes.*)

ANIMAL: Wanker.

CHRISTIAN: Hello. Yeah, ambulance. We got this nutter who's having a heart attack in the Maternity Ward. Cardiff City Peoples'. Yeah, I know it's shut but he's still having a heart attack.

(*QUILLER, still holding the phone, facing LAURA*)

LAURA: Not a lot I can do without a telephone, is there?

QUILLER: Yeah.

LAURA: I don't think so. Now why don't you leave it with me? Your request.

182

QUILLER: So you can bin it.

LAURA: You have my guarantee. It will be dealt with.

(*QUILLER looks at the phone. GILLESPIE comes in.*)

LAURA: Gillespie, can you call Security please.

GILLESPIE: Quiller.

LAURA: Now!

QUILLER: Mister Gillespie.

GILLESPIE: What are you doing here?

QUILLER: Emergency.

LAURA: Gillespie.

GILLESPIE: I could have done with you last night.

QUILLER: Your sort of a date.

GILLESPIE: Dozen roses might have helped.

LAURA: Gillespie.

GILLESPIE: Sorry.

LAURA: I take it you know this gentleman.

GILLESPIE: Everyone knows Quiller.

LAURA: I don't.

GILLESPIE: Well —

LAURA: Well, I'd like him removed.

GILLESPIE: It's only Quiller. He's the flower seller.

QUILLER: Was. How is Interflora?

GILLESPIE: Expensive.

QUILLER: We're free now. Did you get our tender? I told the old man not to write it on that 'with sympathy' card.

GILLESPIE: How is your father?

QUILLER: How you left him. A statistic.

GILLESPIE: That's not true.

LAURA: Gillespie, I am standing here with a vandalised telephone, and I'm afraid I'm not interested in this vandal's father. I am interested in getting this vandal off the premises.

GILLESPIE: Quiller's father was a patient over at the City Hospital.

QUILLER: 'Til you kicked him out.

GILLESPIE: It wasn't like that.

QUILLER: Because he wasn't worth the money.

GILLESPIE: No.

QUILLER: Well, now I've got one who is.

GILLESPIE: What?

QUILLER: Nye Bevan.

LAURA: Mr Gillespie! If you won't listen to my instructions then perhaps you will listen to Mr Quiller's request. He has a patient, a Mr Nye Bevan, installed at the City Peoples' Hospital having a heart attack. He requests two doctors, two nurses, a porter and medication to deal with the emergency. To that end he has forced his way in here, terrorised me and wrenched the telephone from its socket. Now in the light of that information what do you think I should do?

GILLESPIE: I think you should go, Quiller.

LAURA: Gillespie! You stay right where you are.

            (*A phone rings. It is GILLESPIE'S mobile.*)

GILLESPIE: Handy these, aren't they? (*He answers it.*)

LAURA: You're not getting away with this.

QUILLER: Neither are you.

GILLESPIE: Yes, it appears to have been disconnected.

LAURA: It has not been — Gillespie, give me that phone.

GILLESPIE: N. L. Bevan, suspected cardiac — transferred from Cyncoed Court — Cardiff City Peoples' Hospital — lost in transit. Yes, yes, I'll pass it on. (*turns the phone off*)

LAURA: Lost in transit?

GILLESPIE: Well, lost in Maternity actually.

LAURA: What's lost in transit?

GILLESPIE: A patient.

LAURA: A patient? How can you lose a patient?

GILLESPIE: Well, I think they've found him again. Emergency call from the City Hospital. A Mr Bevan. Another heart attack.

LAURA: (*looking out of the window*) I don't believe it.

QUILLER: I gotta go.

LAURA: Bevan. Nye Bevan.

QUILLER: Two doctors. And nurses. Right.

LAURA: Why does that name ring a bell with me?

GILLESPIE: I can't imagine.

QUILLER: You listening to me? If you don't give me what I want, I'll give you what you want. Flowers at midnight. I mean it, Mister Gillespie.

GILLESPIE: Dr Lee, Quiller.

QUILLER: Dr Lee?

GILLESPIE: She's a good doctor. Wish her happy birthday.

QUILLER: Right. Right. (*He goes.*)

GILLESPIE: Take care, Quiller.

LAURA: What did you say?

GILLESPIE: I said "take care".

LAURA: Since when do you say "take care" to departing criminals?

GILLESPIE: It's only Quiller.

LAURA: Who could well be a homicidal maniac. Now can you get on to Security and stop him leaving the building? (*She hands him the telephone, sees the trailing lead.*) Shit. (*throws it down*) And what the hell did he mean "flowers at midnight"?

GILLESPIE: He's a flower seller.

LAURA: Oh, that explains it perfectly. I understand it completely now.

GILLESPIE: Well, I understand it.

LAURA: Do you? Well, do you understand what the hell he was doing in a closed hospital with a private patient having a heart attack? And who the hell is Dr Lee?

GILLESPIE: She's a junior house doctor.

LAURA: So?

GILLESPIE: Well, I don't want to stress you out even more —

LAURA: I am not —

GILLESPIE: Good, because we've lost her as well. Dr Lee. She was the last doctor on call over there. Well, she's disappeared. Sort of.

LAURA: Disappeared. (*She looks across to the hospital.*)

GILLESPIE: I'm not saying she's there. But she was last seen going into the Morgue.

LAURA: The Morgue? And why would a house doctor be visiting the Morgue? Is that the usual part of her rounds?

GILLESPIE: No. But it's — well apparently, it's where they go for — sort of recreational things.

LAURA: What sort of recreational things? (*pause*) I don't want to know, I don't want to know. (*looks across at the hospital again*) All that is ending. All that type of thing will be no more. I thought it was no more. I don't believe this is happening. There should be a salvage firm in there this very minute. But what have I got? A maniac flower seller, a private patient having a heart attack, a junior doctor doing god knows what unspeakable things in the Morgue. You do know I have the prospective developers coming in at twelve?

GILLESPIE: Yeah, could you order me a Big Whoppa please?

LAURA: Gillespie, you are that much away... (*she stops, something clicks*) Bevan. N.L. Bevan. Nye Lloyd Bevan, that's who it is. He's the agent. The agent selling the hospital. That's who I'm meeting this afternoon.

GILLESPIE: Looks like you're meeting him in surgery.

LAURA: It can't be him. It can't.

GILLESPIE: At least he's had a night to have a good look round.

LAURA: Gillespie, I don't think you appreciate that running a hospital is very serious business. And sometimes I don't think you appreciate what that involves.

GILLESPIE: Yeah, I do. It involves doctors and nurses and patients and lots and lots of people like me, who could be absolutely anywhere.

LAURA: Exactly, Gillespie. I suggest you remember that. You could be absolutely anywhere.

GILLESPIE: (*looks across at the hospital*) So could Mr Bevan and Dr Lee.

(*LAURA closes her eyes.*)

GILLESPIE: Sorry. I'll get on to Security. (*He starts to dial the broken phone.*) Stress. It gets to you sometime. Well — not you — (*He dials from the mobile.*)

(*QUILLER'S FATHER sits bolt upright. QUILLER is with him.*)

DAD: He never paid. He never bloody paid.

QUILLER: It's alright, it's alright. Who didn't?

DAD: What do you want?

QUILLER: Are you alright?

DAD: Why? Are you a doctor?

QUILLER: No. No. (*He helps him back down.*) It's going to be alright. It's going to be alright now. He's back. Nye Bevan, he's back.

DAD: He was a big man. Saved your life.

QUILLER: I know. And he can — he can help you now.

DAD: I haven't got beads up my nose, you daft bastard.

QUILLER: No. But he'll make them listen, Dad. They'll sit up and listen now. Make them keep his promise.

DAD: What promise?

QUILLER: What you said, what he promised.... (*stops, looks at his FATHER helplessly*) Don't worry Dad, we're going to sort it. Sort it all out.

DAD: Sort this bed out. It's all over the shop.

(QUILLER *helps him as he starts to drift off again.*)

QUILLER: It's going to be alright. We're going to get you a proper bed. Get you sorted proper.

(*He gets up, starts to go.*)

DAD: Bet he had his bloody fingers crossed.

(QUILLER just looks at him and leaves.)

(ANIMAL and CHRISTIAN are standing over BEVAN.)

CHRISTIAN: Do you think he's dead?

ANIMAL: Definitely. Checked out years ago.

CHRISTIAN: No. Not the one with the bollard on his head. This one.

ANIMAL: Nah. Look at him. He's dreaming.

CHRISTIAN: I think it's dead cruel, that. Calling your kid Nye when your surname's Bevan.

ANIMAL: I don't know.

CHRISTIAN: So you'd like it if your surname had been Kingdom, would you? Animal Kingdom.

ANIMAL: It's not that bad. Now if I'd been called Hospital, I wouldn't have liked that.

CHRISTIAN: Hell, no.

ANIMAL: And what if your surname had been Fundamentalist? Christian Fundamentalist and Animal Hospital.

CHRISTIAN: We would have been jokes.

ANIMAL: Too right. Lucky your name's not Fundamentalist.

CHRISTIAN: And yours isn't Hospital.

ANIMAL: Yeah. But mine's not Animal anyway.

CHRISTIAN: No.

ANIMAL: I bet his name's not Nye Bevan. He's just a nutter.

CHRISTIAN: Unless he is Nye Bevan.

ANIMAL: What? The Nye Bevan

CHRISTIAN: Well, his spirit. Nye Bevan's ghost.

ANIMAL: But if he's a ghost what's he doing having a heart attack?

CHRISTIAN: Well, this is his baby, innit? His creation. And here we are knocking lumps off it. He's not going to be happy about it, is he? Attacking his baby with a chainsaw.

ANIMAL: But what was all that about pasta and Frances and shagging Jackie Kennedy on a motor bike?

CHRISTIAN: Deranged babble of a lost soul. We've wounded his heart, Animal, sent him round the twist.

ANIMAL: I bastard haven't.

CHRISTIAN: Me, you, Mendleson. Someone has.

(*They look at BEVAN, then around the ward.*)

ANIMAL: I've never done a hospital before.

CHRISTIAN: You make it sound like a burglary.

ANIMAL: Well it is, innit? Smash the place up and grab what you can. Pubs, warehouses, offices, big houses, little houses. Loads of little houses. Row after row I've done. Slates, flags, fittings. Peeled 'em bare. And fireplaces. Always fireplaces. And they'd always come out with a groan. Breaking its heart see. Heart of the house.

CHRISTIAN: You're a romantic, Animal.

ANIMAL: A romantic animal. With a chainsaw.

CHRISTIAN: It's a dirty old job.

ANIMAL: But no bastard's got to do it. There's no need for all this shit, is there? So why should anyone have to do it?

CHRISTIAN: People want fireplaces.

ANIMAL: Why?

CHRISTIAN: Lot of broken hearts out there.

ANIMAL: I'm not up for this, I'm really not.

(*QUILLER appears, carrying a takeaway.*)

QUILLER: What are you doing here?

ANIMAL: What the fuck are you doing here?

QUILLER: I'm looking after Mister Bevan.

CHRISTIAN: No, we're looking after Mister Bevan.

QUILLER: Oh, right. Right. Didn't think you'd be this quick.

CHRISTIAN: We're not.

QUILLER: I would have got more.

ANIMAL: Where the hell did you come from?

QUILLER: The Cantonese. In Canton. (*He goes toward BEVAN.*)

CHRISTIAN: You're not allowed to touch him.

QUILLER: No. Right. I've brought him a takeaway. He hasn't eaten.

ANIMAL: You've brought Nye Bevan a Chinese takeaway?

QUILLER: Yeah. Here. (*hands it to him*) What do you want?

ANIMAL: What?

QUILLER: Chinese? Indian?

CHRISTIAN: Chinese.

ANIMAL: Indian.

QUILLER: Right. I'll get a Chinese curry. Won't be long.

(*He goes.*)

ANIMAL: Shit, man shit, who the hell was that? What the fuck's happening?

(*There is the sound of an ambulance siren. BEVAN groans, ANIMAL flips. DAD wakes up.*)

DAD: He's dead, mun. Nye Bevan is dead.

(*Interval.*)

Act Two

(*DR LEE, drifting through the wards.*)

DR. LEE: Beautiful. Absolutely beautiful. Miles and miles of empty beds. Who dreamed this up? I couldn't dream this up. But I could handle this. This, I could deal with. Eight hours in every one. Eight unbroken hours. Perhaps a consultation here and there, and then — and then, back to bed. Must still be my birthday. This is how it should be. Does anyone know how it should be? This'll do. This'll do for me. For now. Just for today. (*She moves on.*)

(*The same paramedic comes in to Maternity wheeling his stretcher.*)

DEREK: I am not responsible. No one can say I am responsible.

ANIMAL: I can.

CHRISTIAN: And me. It's easy.

BOTH: I am responsible.

ANIMAL: See.

DEREK: Who are you? (*sees the tools*) What are you doing here?

CHRISTIAN: We're in charge of Nye Bevan's ghost.

DEREK: What? Oh God. How long? (*He starts to check NYE'S pulse and his breathing.*)

ANIMAL: No idea. Ages, I suppose.

DEREK: Oh Jesus.

CHRISTIAN: I'd say it's probably been twenty years. Perhaps longer.

ANIMAL: Easy.

DEREK: What? This man's pulse is very near normal.

ANIMAL: What's normal? Mine sometimes goes at two hundred rpm and look at me.

DEREK: He seems fine. Absolutely fine. Well, stable anyway.

CHRISTIAN: Thank god for that, a stable ghost.

ANIMAL: Yeah, we thought he might be nuts.

DEREK: Who are you two, anyway?

ANIMAL: Animal Hospital.

CHRISTIAN: And Christian Fundamentalist.

ANIMAL: Don't laugh.

DEREK: You shouldn't be here.

ANIMAL: Excuse me Pal, I don't want to be here but we've got every right to be here. It's this poor bastard who shouldn't be here.

CHRISTIAN: If it wasn't for us the National Health would have a dead ghost on its hands.

DEREK: He's a private patient, actually.

CHRISTIAN: You mean he's paying for this? Paying good money to be dumped in a derelict hospital at the mercy of nutters with chainsaws?

DEREK: He was not dumped.

ANIMAL: What sort of person would do that?

CHRISTIAN: An animal.

DEREK: Look —

ANIMAL: That's not fair.

CHRISTIAN: Sorry, Animal.

ANIMAL: Worse than an animal.

DEREK: Listen —

CHRISTIAN: A barbarian.

ANIMAL: A psycho barbarian.

DEREK: Will you listen —

CHRISTIAN: A psycho killer barbarian.

ANIMAL: Yeah, a psycho killer barbarian would leave someone like this.

DEREK: I did not leave him like this.

CHRISTIAN: So it was you.

ANIMAL: You bastard.

DEREK: I did leave him. Which I was contracted to do. But not like this.

ANIMAL: So what was he like, then? Shagging his way through a ward of nurses, was he?

DEREK: He was in good hands.

CHRISTIAN: Whose?

DEREK: I left him with two midwives.

CHRISTIAN: You left a man having a heart attack with two midwives? What sort of health worker are you?

DEREK: I am a paramedic.

ANIMAL: Bastard paratrooper more like. Take no prisoners.

DEREK: I was doing my job.

CHRISTIAN: You're unfit.

DEREK: A very difficult job. And it wasn't just two midwives, there was another man here.

CHRISTIAN: Who was that, then? That man they hire to saw people's legs off, was it?

DEREK: It was a man of authority. A man I could trust.

ANIMAL: Not a paramedic then.

DEREK: And what do you know about paramedics?

CHRISTIAN: Well, they get to wear those nice green combat suits.

ANIMAL: And rush through crowds telling people to get back.

CHRISTIAN: And scream through red lights making everyone else mount the pavements.

ANIMAL: Pretty cool, really.

DEREK: Oh yes, dead cool. Flashing lights and sirens. That's all you see is the glamour, isn't it? Like everyone else all you see is the bloody glamour. You think it's all sex, drugs and rock 'n roll.

CHRISTIAN: Is it?

DEREK: No, it's not. I don't see lights and sirens. All I see are targets and quotas and deadlines and time bloody limits. And somewhere under that pile of crap are patients. Patients. That I'm supposed to be caring for. Do you understand what I'm saying? Do you hear what I'm saying?

CHRISTIAN: We hear you, we hear you.

DEREK: I used to care about what I do, now I do what I don't care about.

CHRISTIAN: Sorry.

ANIMAL: Aye, sorry man. We been a bit spooked.

DEREK: How do you think he feels? My patient? Now can you move those things, please? I do have a job to do. Enough to give anyone a heart attack.

CHRISTIAN: Right.

             (*DEREK starts to move BEVAN onto the stretcher.*)

ANIMAL: Here, I'll give you a hand. I'm good at this.

DEREK: He is a patient, not a sack of shit.

ANIMAL: Sorry.

(*BEVAN lets out a groan, then a yell.*)

DEREK: It's alright Mr Bevan, we'll soon have you in good hands.

BEVAN: Keep away from me. Murderer. Keep that bloody murderer away from me.

ANIMAL: This is getting seriously heavy.

(*DR LEE, still on the wards, is confronted by QUILLER.*)

QUILLER: Doctor Lee? It is Doctor Lee, isn't it?

DR. LEE: I — yes, yes it is.

QUILLER: Happy birthday.

DR. LEE: Yes, yes it is. Was. How —

QUILLER: From Mister Gillespie. He says you're a good doctor.

DR. LEE: Am I? I wouldn't know. Shouldn't you be in bed?

QUILLER: No, that's Nye Bevan. He's waiting for you.

DR. LEE: Nye Bevan is waiting for me?

QUILLER: Yeah, I'm getting food. I didn't get you anything. What do you want, Chinese or Indian?

DR. LEE: Chips. I could kill a bag of chips.

QUILLER: Chips. I didn't think doctors ate chips.

DR. LEE: They probably don't.

QUILLER: Right. Right. Be back as soon as I can. (*He goes.*)

DR. LEE: Mr Gillespie thinks I'm a good doctor, does he? (*walks on*)

(*BEVAN is clinging to his bed.*)

ANIMAL: How about a takeaway, Mister Bevan?

BEVAN: Just take him away. Take him right away from me.

DEREK: Calm down Mr Bevan, you're not doing yourself any good.

BEVAN: And what good are you going to do me? He tried to kill me. He's the idiot that left me here. Him and that flower seller.

CHRISTIAN: Flower seller?

ANIMAL: A man of authority?

CHRISTIAN: A man you could trust?

DEREK: He's not just a flower seller.

CHRISTIAN: You left him with a flower seller and two mid-wives.

DEREK: It was an emergency.

BEVAN: Yes, I was bloody dying.

DEREK: You weren't dying.

BEVAN: Well, I'm dying now. I want to die now. I want to die here, so bugger off the lot of you.

ANIMAL: You can't die in Maternity, it's not right.

BEVAN: Will you stop saying that. Can't you just let a man die without stripping him of his dignity?

DEREK: No one is going to die, Mr Bevan.

BEVAN: We all are, you stupid bugger. And this is my moment. I've had the calling card. Do you know Frances didn't even send me a card.

ANIMAL: Who's Frances?

BEVAN: She's a beautiful woman. Looks like Jackie Kennedy, you know. Gave me Chianti and grilled red — and what did I give her? Nothing, except stress. I deserve this. I deserve to die here, alone and wretched.

DEREK: You're not going to die.

BEVAN: I want to die. She might send me a bloody card then. When they find my broken body. Lonely estate agent, abandoned, deserted, left to rot in some — where the hell am I anyway?

DEREK: You're in the City Peoples' Hospital in the — well in one of the wards.

BEVAN: The where?

ANIMAL: Cardiff City Peoples' Hospital. Except it's got no people in it.

BEVAN: I'm supposed to be here.

DEREK: No, you're not supposed to be here.

BEVAN: I am. I am. I'm bloody well supposed to be here. Today. At twelve.

CHRISTIAN: No. We're supposed to be here today.

ANIMAL: Gutting the place.

BEVAN: And I'm supposed to be selling the place.

ANIMAL: You're selling a hospital?

CHRISTIAN: You can't sell a hospital.

BEVAN: Exactly, exactly. It can't be done. But that's what I have to do. This is the sort of job they expect me to do. Sell this place so it can be turned into — and if I bugger it up, and I musn't bugger it up, and Jesus, I have buggered it up.

CHRISTIAN: So you're buggered.

BEVAN: Jesus Christ, what the hell is happening?

DEREK: It's a mistake, that's all. Computer error.

BEVAN: No, no, this is no mistake, this is fate. Do you believe in fate?

ANIMAL: No, it's all bollocks, if it was meant to happen it was meant to happen, that's what I think.

BEVAN: This was meant to happen, believe me. This is my fate, my destiny for not giving a shit.

ANIMAL: I'm not with you.

BEVAN: Frances is with me. She'd understand what's going on. She could see this coming.

DEREK: Heart attacks are very difficult to —

BEVAN: Do you ever have that dream that you're visiting your wife's or your girlfriend's parents and as you get out of the car to walk up the drive you suddenly realise you're only wearing a vest. A dirty, child's vest that you had when you were eight.

CHRISTIAN: Never.

BEVAN: Well this is for real. Because at twelve o'clock my career will be hanging by a thread and resting on my virtuoso performance and look at me. I haven't had a wash, I haven't had a shave, I've probably pissed myself and I'm on my nineteenth heart attack. Wonderful, absolutely bloody wonderful. It's not fate, it's hubris that's what it is.

ANIMAL: That is real nasty shit.

BEVAN: Get me out of here. You've got to get me out of here.

CHRISTIAN: Oi. I thought you wanted to die.

BEVAN: No one wants to die.

ANIMAL: You did. Alone and wretched.

BEVAN: No. That's what I have been, alone and wretched.

Frances would tell you. Well, I'm not going to die of humiliation, that's for sure. (*He gets out of bed.*)

DEREK: That's the spirit, Mr Bevan.

BEVAN: No, this is fate snatching me from the flames. I've needed this to take a raincheck on life. I've just been one flicker away from burn out.

ANIMAL: I'm sure Nye Bevan never talked bollocks like this.

BEVAN: (*grabbing hold of him*) That man. That name, was hung around my neck by my sick bloody father. It's nothing to do with me. And I'm nothing to do with it, him, or its sick, wet nurse memory. Everything I've done, I've done by myself for myself. Without the help of anyone. Right?

ANIMAL: Right. You'll be making your own way to the hospital then.

BEVAN: I have paid for this.

ANIMAL: No. We've paid for this. You ain't got your greasy hot dog fingers on it yet.

DEREK: Let's not agitate the patient, shall we? (*transfers him to the stretcher*)

BEVAN: Yes, I need calm and rest. They can't blame me for having a heart attack.

DEREK: No one's going to blame you. You're going to be looked after. Professional medical care.

CHRISTIAN: Listen to Florence fucking Nightingale. Where you going to dump him next?

ANIMAL: They're shutting down Kwiksave, try the cold store there.

DEREK: It's a wonderful new hospital, Mr Bevan.

CHRISTIAN: It's a fucking airport.

BEVAN: How can anyone sell this place? Look at it. It's

	falling to bits.
ANIMAL:	Eh, we haven't started yet.
BEVAN:	Well, do your worst.

(*DEREK starts to wheel him out. He is confronted by DR LEE.*)

DR. LEE:	And where do you think you're going?
BEVAN:	Out.
DR. LEE:	You're certainly not. Now back into bed immediately.
BEVAN:	What?
DEREK:	I'm transferring him, Doctor. Down to City New — where did you come from?
DR. LEE:	Do you know what? In this endless year I have carried out this endless trek around endless wards looking at endless patients, and no one has ever asked me that. They all think I'm there just for them, in their own little sphere. Well today Mr... (*She looks at his chart.*) Bevan, this is your lucky day because I'm here just for you. Now hop back into bed.
BEVAN:	What are you talking about? It's shut. The bloody place is shut. There's no one here.
DR. LEE:	No, I'm here Mr Bevan, you're in very good hands.
DEREK:	Doctor, he's had a heart attack.
DR. LEE:	Well he doesn't want to be running around then, does he?
DEREK:	You don't understand, I am transferring him.
DR. LEE:	I don't understand? I understand that I am a doctor and you are an ambulance driver. Now I won't tell you how to take bends at fifty, so don't tell me how to treat patients. Now into bed with him.

BEVAN: I am not getting into that bed. No bloody way.

DR. LEE: Nurse. Get him in please.

(*CHRISTIAN and ANIMAL look at one another.*)

DEREK: Nurse?

DR. LEE: Whatever they are. Get him in.

ANIMAL: Whatever you say, Doctor.

CHRISTIAN: Yo.

(*They lift him in.*)

BEVAN: I am not staying in this place any longer. Are you listening to me? This is bloody ridiculous. I can't stay here, I can't. Oh Jesus Christ, this can't be happening, it can't. It's a nightmare, a bloody nightmare, it's got to be.

DR. LEE: No, no, quite the opposite, Mr Bevan.

(*The Executive Office. LAURA is peering through binoculars. GILLESPIE is on the phone.*)

LAURA: I don't believe it. I just do not believe it.

GILLESPIE: (*putting the phone down*) No. Nor me.

LAURA: What's he doing in there, performing heart surgery?

GILLESPIE: Perhaps he can't get through the crowds.

LAURA: (*She tosses the glasses to GILLESPIE.*) They're useless, Gillespie. Can't see a damn thing.

GILLESPIE: They're not meant for that. They're for the theatre. When I used to go out.

LAURA: That's your trouble, you should go out more. What crowds?

GILLESPIE: Well, not exactly crowds.

LAURA: Well, exactly what then?

GILLESPIE: Well, I can't say exactly, but security say there's a bit of a fuss over there.

(*He looks through the glasses.*)

LAURA: What fuss? There's no fuss. There's just a man having a heart attack.

GILLESPIE: Well, apparently there's a rumour that we've left a load of dead people over there. It's causing a bit of a stink.

LAURA: Dead people? A bit of a stink? (*She grabs the glasses.*) We do not want crowds, Gillespie. I want them moved and I want them moved now. What the hell are Security doing?

GILLESPIE: They refuse to touch the place. They say there's screams and yells coming from there.

(*She stares at him.*)

LAURA: It's that junior doctor, that's what it is. Jumped up bloody student on some drunken prank. Shouldn't be let near a hospital.

GILLESPIE: Be nice if she was let out now and then though.

LAURA: What's that supposed to mean? Don't you try and tell me about doctors, Gillespie.

GILLESPIE: No. You can't trust 'em, can you?

LAURA: Seven years training, thirty grand a year and they're still clueless.

GILLESPIE: Don't know the Morgue from Maternity, do they?

LAURA: Exactly. (*stops, stares at him*) Do you know something I don't, Gillespie?

GILLESPIE: Doubt it.

LAURA: (*She grabs the glasses again.*) What is going on over there? And what about that damn flower seller?

Have they found him yet?

GILLESPIE: No, but they know where he's been.

LAURA: I know where he's been. Left his calling card, didn't he?

GILLESPIE: He did at Maternity too. And at Casualty and the Children's Ward. He's been giving flowers away. Says they're on the NHS.

LAURA: He says they're on the NHS?

GILLESPIE: Yes, remember that?

LAURA: Don't be funny.

GILLESPIE: Oh, and he left a message at reception, asking why we haven't got a Geriatric Ward. They couldn't tell him.

LAURA: Gillespie, I want that man — I want that man....

(*She suddenly loses her breath and holds her chest.*)

GILLESPIE: Are you alright?

LAURA: Asthma attack.

GILLESPIE: Shall I crank up the internet?

LAURA: Get my inhaler, you bloody fool.

(*He gets it, she sucks in deeply. MENDLESON comes in.*)

MEN.: Good morning. Not a good morning though, is it? Not a good morning all round by the looks of things.

GILLESPIE: I'm sorry, I don't....

MEN.: Mendleson. As in salvage. Having a slight pulmonary problem, are we? We're having a pulmonary problem over there too. Not that slight though.

GILLESPIE: It's just a touch of asthma.

205

MEN.: Well, he says it's a heart attack. Oh I'm sorry, you mean....

GILLESPIE: This isn't really a very good time.

MEN.: No, no. My brother suffered from asthma for years. Turned out to be lung cancer, had it cut away. No problem now.

LAURA: (*struggling with her breath*) Mr Mendleson.

MEN.: Laura. You did say I could call you Laura, didn't you?

LAURA: No, I didn't. What do you want, Mr Mendleson?

MEN.: I want some assurances, Laura. A guarantee.

LAURA: You have a guarantee, Mr Mendleson, which is non-negotiable.

MEN.: I believe we were talking architectural salvage. I didn't expect to find phantom patients crawling out of the woodwork.

LAURA: How do you mean, patients?

GILLESPIE: How do you mean, phantom?

LAURA: I'm dealing with this, Gillespie.

GILLESPIE: I thought you were having an asthma attack.

LAURA: Yes and I'm dealing with that as well. (*takes another suck*) Now you said patients, Mr Mendleson, are you implying that there are more than one?

MEN.: You tell me.

LAURA: I will tell you. I am telling you. I'm telling you there's one. Mr Bevan. And he shouldn't be there.

GILLESPIE: Well he should. But he's a bit early.

LAURA: Gillespie, can you please get on to Security?

MEN.: I mean, if we've found a man in Maternity what

are we going to find in the Morgue?

GILLESPIE: Well —

LAURA: Nothing.

(*GILLESPIE moves to the phone. It rings. He answers it.*)

MEN.: I will be looking at compensation.

LAURA: For what?

MEN.: Stress. My employees have been severely traumatised. Can you imagine what it's like to walk into an empty hospital to be confronted with a madman in Maternity screaming he's having a heart attack and claiming to be Nye Bevan?

LAURA: But he is.

MEN.: What?

LAURA: He is Nye Bevan. (*MENDLESON looks suitably bemused.*) And he's probably having a heart attack. Now those are the facts, I'm sorry if you don't like them.

(*MENDLESON struggles for an answer. GILLESPIE comes off the phone.*)

LAURA: Right, Gillespie, is everything clear so Mr Mendleson can get on?

GILLESPIE: Well the ambulance driver has called to say he can't get in and the paramedic is not coming out.

LAURA: What?

GILLESPIE: The ambulance driver —

LAURA: Gillespie, can you start talking sense please?

GILLESPIE: That's what he says. No one wants to go in and no one wants to come out. Apparently.

MEN.: There's something funny going on over there.

207

LAURA: There is nothing funny going on — have you spoken to Security? What are they doing?

GILLESPIE: They're um... they're handing out flowers.

MEN.:   Right. I want my men out.

LAURA: Handing out — it's that bloody flower seller.

GILLESPIE: They probably knew his father. Everyone knew his father. Everyone knew Quiller.

LAURA: I don't know him.

GILLESPIE: He's been very ill.

LAURA: Gillespie, I'd like you to cancel that meeting this afternoon.

MEN.:   I've got a contract, Laura.

LAURA: Gillespie, can you do that now please?

GILLESPIE: We wouldn't treat him. We could have treated him. Said he was too old.

LAURA: I am talking to you, Gillespie.

GILLESPIE: Could have given him a few more months. Perhaps more. Been here longer than anyone. Well, been over there longer than anyone. Don't know how he made a living. Don't know how he kept going.

LAURA: Gillespie.

GILLESPIE: And now we've killed him off.

LAURA: In case you haven't noticed Gillespie, there has been a breach of security —

MEN.:   There has been a breach of contract.

LAURA: And I think we should do something about it.

GILLESPIE: There has been a breach of contract.

MEN.:   There.

(He takes the glasses and looks across to the hospital.)

LAURA: Right. I'll cancel the meeting, shall I?

(She gets hold of the mobile.)

MEN.: You want to get that bloke out of there first.

LAURA: Good idea. I'll get on to that as well.

MEN.: You need a direct line through to that paramedic, that's the best route.

LAURA: Yes, dealing with that straight away, then perhaps I should scrub up and get ready for surgery. Gillespie!

GILLESPIE: What?

LAURA: How do I get through to Emergency?

GILLESPIE: Dial 999.

LAURA: This is serious.

GILLESPIE: I know. It's an emergency.

LAURA: Well, do something.

GILLESPIE: Like what?

LAURA: Like your job.

GILLESPIE: Fuck my job.

LAURA: Gillespie, I didn't hear you say that.

GILLESPIE: No, I know you didn't. Because you are one deaf bitch.

LAURA: I am not deaf.

GILLESPIE: No, and you're not blind either and you still can't see what's happening.

(He looks out of the window.)

MEN.: So what is? Happening.

GILLESPIE: I don't know. I don't know yet. But something is.

(There is a voice on the mobile.)

LAURA: Yes. No. No, I do not want the fire service. I want, I want — *(she begins to lose her breath)* Gillespie. Gillespie. How the hell do you get through to anyone in this place?

(GILLESPIE looks at her for a moment then takes the phone.)

(There is a yell from BEVAN. DR LEE is checking his blood pressure. ANIMAL is squirting a syringe which he has taken from DEREK'S bag.)

BEVAN: For Christ's sake, will someone take that off him?

ANIMAL: *(giving it another squirt)* What's this one do then?

DR. LEE: It's useless. Tried it a couple of times. It just sends you to sleep.

BEVAN: I do not want to go to sleep. I do not want to be here.

DR. LEE: 'Course you don't.

DEREK: He should not be touching that equipment.

DR. LEE: Sorry, nurse.

DEREK: I am not a nurse.

CHRISTIAN: *(holding up a defibrillator)* Where do you stick this?

DEREK: Will you put that back?

DR. LEE: OK boys, probably not a good idea, you know what these ambulance drivers are like.

DEREK: I am not an —

DR. LEE: Sorry, you're not an ambulance driver. What exactly are you then?

ANIMAL: He's a paramedic.

DR. LEE: So that'll be higher than a nurse.

CHRISTIAN: But lower than a flower seller.

DR. LEE: That'll make you a consultant. There you are Mr Bevan, nothing to worry about, your own personal consultant.

DEREK: I am not a consultant. I am a paramedic.

BEVAN: And he's taking me to hospital, so why don't you let him?

DR. LEE: This is a hospital, Mr Bevan. Or can I call you Nye?

BEVAN: No you bloody can't. Now take me to the New.

DR. LEE: I don't know why you want to go there.

BEVAN: Because I'm bloody having a heart attack.

DR. LEE: (*looking at the pressure reading*) Don't think so.

BEVAN: What do you mean, don't think so? Why do you think I'm lying here like this?

DR. LEE: Stressed out?

BEVAN: I am not stressed out.

CHRISTIAN: No, he's bastard hyper, he's got to sell this hospital by twelve.

DR. LEE: You can't sell a hospital.

BEVAN: I know, I know, so can you please get me out of here?

DEREK: I really think I should transfer him Doctor, I can't leave him here again.

BEVAN: No, you damn well can't, and I'm paying so I can go where I like.

DR. LEE: Oh you're paying, are you?

BEVAN: Yes I am, and before you say it doesn't make a difference, I know it does.

CHRISTIAN: Yeah, look at that, your blood pressure's doubled.

211

DR. LEE: Well, it is a little high. A private patient with a heart complaint. I'm going to have to keep you under very strict observation.

DEREK: Doctor, he can't stay here. I can't stay here.

BEVAN: Don't you leave me here again, you swine.

DR. LEE: Quite right, where's your sense of professional conduct? You stay here where you're needed.

(*DEREK looks around desperately.*)

DEREK: It's an empty hospital. It's shut. What you going to do? What is he going to do?

DR. LEE: Well first of all he can cut out stress, red meat and alcohol.

ANIMAL: What about drugs?

DR. LEE: What have you got?

ANIMAL: Anything you like.

DR. LEE: There you are. Everything the doctor orders.

BEVAN: This is a joke. Some terrible practical joke.

DR. LEE: I think it's better to look at it as a warning. An amber light to your lifestyle. You'd probably be better off being a woman as well. Less risk.

BEVAN: What sort of doctor are you?

DR. LEE: I don't know. I don't know. I've never had the chance to find out. Never had the time to find out.

BEVAN: Well, you're not finding out on me.

(*He starts to get out, falls to the floor. ANIMAL and CHRISTIAN put him back in.*)

CHRISTIAN: Perhaps you should listen to the doctor.

DR. LEE: Perhaps you should. Because I might be a very good doctor. I might be a brilliant doctor.

Nobody knows, nobody probably cares. But I care. But I don't know, because at the moment I'm up to my eyeballs in morphine and vodka with one solitary and private patient. Which makes me a very, very happy doctor.

ANIMAL: Wow.

BEVAN: Shit.

CHRISTIAN: Scary or what? Nye Bevan's ghost and a sky high doctor.

ANIMAL: Wow.

DEREK: Jesus Christ.

DR. LEE: Now I suggest we all relax. Chill out, Mr Bevan. No worries.

BEVAN: Oh shit.

              (*DEREK'S mobile rings.*)

DR. LEE: That is yours. That is not mine. Mine is dead, drowned, lost at sea and at rest in the Morgue.

DEREK: Hello. Yes. Yes. No.

ANIMAL: Fuck fireplaces. This is the business.

CHRISTIAN: Something else.

DR. LEE: Headache. Bit of a headache. (*She takes out her bottle which is empty.*) Shit.

              (*QUILLER comes in. He is carrying some takeaways.*)

DEREK: Yes, yes, he seems to be alright. Yes, she is here, but, well, she seems to be —

              (*QUILLER takes the phone.*)

QUILLER: I think that's for me. Yes, everything seems fine. But you seem to have got the order mixed up. I ordered two doctors, two nurses and one porter. You seem to have sent me one doctor, one nurse and two porters. But I think we can live with it.

I'll get back to you on the drugs. (*He hands the phone back to DEREK.*) Hello. I'm Quiller. The flower seller.

CHRISTIAN: The man of authority.

ANIMAL: The man you can trust.

BEVAN: No. No, no, no, no, no.

QUILLER: How are you Mister Bevan? How was the Chinese?

(*GILLESPIE puts the phone down.*)

GILLESPIE: Two porters, one nurse, one doctor, one patient and an ambulance in waiting. They're better equipped than us. Oh and a flower seller.

MEN.: Two porters?

GILLESPIE: Normal service is restored.

MEN.: Are you trying to tell me that the hospital is still open?

GILLESPIE: Well someone's trying to tell us.

MEN.: Two porters.

GILLESPIE: And a doctor and an ambulance. Looks like a hijack. Your move, I believe. (*LAURA is staring into space.*) Laura? The flower seller has got his doctor and a nurse and an ambulance.

MEN.: And two bloody porters.

GILLESPIE: I think we have a little local difficulty. Laura?

LAURA: Normal service.

GILLESPIE: What?

LAURA: As you say, normal service is restored. Carry on, Mr Mendleson.

MEN.: Carry on?

GILLESPIE: What about Nye Bevan?

LAURA: I do not need Nye Bevan. Nye Bevan is not selling the hospital. I am.

GILLESPIE: I meant Nye Bevan the patient.

LAURA: Yes, exactly. Nye Bevan the patient is receiving normal service. Nothing more we can do. But carry on.

GILLESPIE: As if nothing is happening?

LAURA: Nothing is happening, Gillespie.

GILLESPIE: But they've got —

LAURA: As far as it affects us Gillespie, nothing is happening.

GILLESPIE: There you are Mr Mendleson, you just cut and hack away as if nothing is happening, no one will notice, we've been doing it for years.

LAURA: Gillespie, I have been doing everyone else's dirty work for a lot longer than that, and I don't need you to show me how to run this hospital and I don't need Mr Bevan to help me sell that hospital. I can do it myself. I don't need anyone.

(*Her breath catches her again.*)

MEN.:   You need a —

LAURA: And I do not need a damn doctor. Thank you, Mr Mendleson. Keep me posted.

(*He edges out.*)

GILLESPIE: I'll get a doctor.

(*He starts to dial. She cuts him off.*)

LAURA: Over my dead body.

(*ANIMAL, CHRISTIAN and DR LEE are digging*

into the food.)

BEVAN: This, is not real.

ANIMAL: I tell you what, this vindaloo is blinding, you want to get some down you, Mr Bevan.

BEVAN: It's not happening.

QUILLER: Mister Bevan's got heart disease, he should avoid cholesterol.

DEREK: And you'd know, would you?

QUILLER: I've worked here for a long time. My father's worked here a long time.

DEREK: You're a bloody flower seller.

ANIMAL: Yeah, the man of authority, the man you could trust. Remember?

DEREK: I was just doing my job.

QUILLER: Yeah, he was. Now we all are. A doctor, a nurse, two porters and Nye Bevan.

               (*They look at each other uncertainly.*)

BEVAN: No. No, no, bloody no.

QUILLER: It's alright Mister Bevan, there's a doctor here now, isn't there?

DR. LEE: Yes. Yes, there's a doctor here.

QUILLER: Good to have a doctor in the hospital. Well of course it's good. It's obvious, innit?

DR. LEE: Good to have a flower seller. All good hospitals have flowers.

QUILLER: That's what my father used to say. Still does.

BEVAN: Are you listening to me? This isn't happening, this should not be happening.

DEREK: I'm listening Mr Bevan, this should definitely not be happening and it's nothing to do with me.

BEVAN: It's everything to do with you. You, this nutter and this flaming quack.

DR. LEE: I don't think it's wise to start abusing your doctor, Mr Bevan.

ANIMAL: And you better not start on the porters either.

QUILLER: It was meant to happen.

ANIMAL: Yeah, yeah, that's what I said, what's meant to happen is meant to happen.

CHRISTIAN: What? What's meant to happen?

QUILLER: Him. Nye Bevan. Turning up here.

BEVAN: I am not Nye Bevan.

QUILLER: I know. I know you're not.

BEVAN: Well, there you are then.

QUILLER: But you're still someone called Nye Bevan who's turned up on the steps and met a flower seller called Quiller on the night this hospital closed. Just like a man called Nye Bevan turned up on these steps and met a flower seller called Quiller on the day this hospital opened.

BEVAN: So?

ANIMAL: So your number's marked, innit? It's obvious.

BEVAN: Marked for what?

QUILLER: Marked to be here.

BEVAN: You're mad, you're barking mad. And I am having a heart attack, for god's sake.

QUILLER: I'm not mad. I'm tamping.

BEVAN: Well I'm not mad either, I'm just, I'm just — Oh Jesus Christ Frances, where are you?

CHRISTIAN: He's just someone called Nye Bevan.

BEVAN: Yes.

ANIMAL: By his sick bloody father.

BEVAN: Yes.

CHRISTIAN: Hung round his neck.

BEVAN: Bloody yes.

ANIMAL: Nothing to do with him.

CHRISTIAN: He's done it all himself.

BEVAN: Yes.

ANIMAL: On his tod.

CHRISTIAN: Big meeting at twelve.

ANIMAL: Selling the hospital.

BEVAN: No.

CHRISTIAN: In his dirty old vest.

ANIMAL: He's buggered it up.

CHRISTIAN: His wife's pissed off.

BEVAN: No.

ANIMAL: And he's pissed himself.

CHRISTIAN: He was meant to be here.

ANIMAL: He said so himself.

BEVAN: I know, I know, I know. Oh Jesus Christ, somebody help me.

QUILLER: We are, Mr Bevan. Trust us. We've got a doctor. You can trust a doctor.

BEVAN: I don't trust anyone.

DR. LEE: I think you should calm down Mr Bevan, take it easy.

ANIMAL: Just chill out, you're in a stress free zone.

BEVAN: Look, can you just take me away from here, just take me away so I can — so I can just....

QUILLER: So you can just die.

DR. LEE: You're not going to die Mr Bevan, I'm not going to let you die. You're my patient.

BEVAN: I am dead. I'm dead already.

CHRISTIAN: Because you can't sell a hospital?

BEVAN: How can anyone sell this? No one could sell this. I couldn't. I haven't sold anything for months. I'd have to give it away. They know that. They knew. You can't sell a hospital.

QUILLER: 'Course you can't. Nye Bevan could have told you that, your father could have —

             (*BEVAN lurches out of bed and grabs QUILLER by the collar.*)

BEVAN: My father couldn't tell me anything, he doesn't speak to me and I don't speak to him.

QUILLER: You don't speak to your father? And you want to die. You might die. My father don't speak to me. I don't want him to die. But he will die.

BEVAN: That's not my bloody fault! (*He lets him go.*) Sorry. Sorry.

QUILLER: You will be. When you don't die and he does.

BEVAN: Look, you don't know what it's like, trying to sell property when you're called Nye Bevan. He's the man who gave the country a national institution, I'm the guy selling a two room flat in Grangetown.

ANIMAL: I thought you were selling a hospital.

BEVAN: (*turning on ANIMAL*) You can't sell a hospital. I can't sell anything. Not a bloody thing. Look at me. I'm pathetic. I'm useless. I'm absolutely fucking useless. And do you know something else? I don't want to sell anything, I wasn't meant to sell anything and I definitely wasn't meant to

219

sell hospitals. In fact no one — I repeat — no one was meant to sell hospitals.

(*A fairly stunned silence as BEVAN, now beside himself, is probably astride the bed.*)

ANIMAL: All he needs now is a bollard on his head.

BEVAN: What?

ANIMAL: Your old man was on the ball calling you Nye Bevan.

CHRISTIAN: You're in the wrong job.

BEVAN: I am, I am. (*looks around him*) I bloody am.

QUILLER: Your old man would be proud of you.

BEVAN: My old man — my father — my old man — I'm not the Nye Bevan he wants me to be.

CHRISTIAN: But you're still Nye Bevan.

(*BEVAN weighs this up.*)

DR. LEE: Trouble is, you're not a patient either.

BEVAN: I am.

DR. LEE: No, you're not. There's nothing wrong with you.

BEVAN: I've had a heart attack. I've been having them all night.

DR. LEE: Then you must have the heart of an ox, look at you. (*He's still on the bed.*) And I bet your blood pressure hasn't blown a bubble, hasn't all day.

BEVAN: But you said —

DR. LEE: You're a dream, Mr Bevan, a junior house doctor's dream. And either the morphine's worn off, or I've just woken up. (*She screws up her bag of chips.*)

BEVAN: But I've been in agony. Sheer agony for hours.

DR. LEE: You and me both. Stress, Mr Bevan, stress. We've

	pigged out on it.
BEVAN:	Stress?
DR. LEE:	Yeah. Try swapping it for sex. I seem to remember that doing the trick. For a bit.
QUILLER:	He's alright?
DR. LEE:	As alright as any of us.
BEVAN:	There's nothing wrong with me?
DR. LEE:	Well, there's nothing I can do.
BEVAN:	So can I go?

(*They all look at one another.*)

ANIMAL:	But I want to be a porter.
DR. LEE:	I want you to be a porter. I want to be a doctor. And I want Mr Bevan to be our patient. One patient. One bed. No buzzer. Bliss. Morphine bliss.
QUILLER:	But you're meant to be here.
DR. LEE:	There's nothing for us to do. And that's not how it should be. It's just how I want it to be.
DEREK:	Right. (*starts to pack his bag*) Time is money, as they say.
DR. LEE:	I must be in the wrong job.
ANIMAL:	Who isn't?

(*They start to go.*)

QUILLER:	No. No. You're a doctor, you're a good doctor. Mister Gillespie said. So you've got to stay.
DR. LEE:	Mr. Gillespie —
QUILLER:	(*picking up a chainsaw and standing in front of them*) No. You're not going.
ANIMAL:	Eh, Quiller man.

QUILLER: Mister Gillespie said I could trust you. Lying, was he? Mister Gillespie lying about you, was he? I don't know, you tell me, because I don't bloody know. Is Mister Gillespie a liar like all the rest of them?

(*GILLESPIE is at the screen. LAURA is sitting down, not looking well.*)

GILLESPIE: I don't know why I'm doing this.

LAURA: It's your job.

GILLESPIE: I'm not a doctor.

LAURA: Look under diaphragm.

GILLESPIE: You're not having a stitch.

LAURA: You're not a doctor.

GILLESPIE: No, but the hospital's full of them.

LAURA: Diaphragm, diaphragm. (*She looks seriously short of breath.*)

GILLESPIE: This is ridiculous. I am getting a doctor now.

LAURA: Gillespie! I am the Chief Executive and I will not be a patient in my own hospital.

GILLESPIE: You need a doctor.

LAURA: I don't need a doctor, I don't want a doctor and I definitely don't... (*Her breath stops her.*)

GILLESPIE: Trust a doctor.

(*QUILLER and DR LEE.*)

DR. LEE: Mr Gillespie is not a liar.

QUILLER: Well then?

DR. LEE: What do you want me to do?

QUILLER: You're a doctor. And I've got a patient.

DR. LEE: But he's alright, Quiller.

QUILLER: Not him. My father.

DR. LEE: Your father?

QUILLER: He needs chemotherapy. He's waiting to come in. That's why you're here.

DR. LEE: Now Mr Quiller, hold on.

QUILLER: He's dying and he needs chemotherapy.

DR. LEE: Quiller —

QUILLER: Are you a doctor or what?

DR. LEE: Well, yes —

QUILLER: Well, I've got a patient.

DR. LEE: Quiller, I can't —

QUILLER: Can't, won't, wouldn't. That's what you mean. That's what they said. My father is dying and he needs treatment. And they wouldn't give it — kicked him out, killed him off. Because he's too fucking old. They promised. You all made promises. You, Mister Gillespie, them over there and you're all going to fucking break 'em. You promised Mister Bevan. On the steps. From the cradle to the grave. And now you've come back, you've got to keep it. You've got to make them keep your promise. Because I don't want him to die. He's not ready. I'm not ready. That's why you're all here, can't you see? Tell her, Mister Bevan, tell 'em all.

(*BEVAN looks helplessly at DR LEE.*)

ANIMAL: I'll tell them. I'll tell the bastards. Whoever they are. You bring your old man here, Quiller. Dr. Lee will look after him.

CHRISTIAN: He can't come here.

ANIMAL: Why not? It's a hospital, innit?

DEREK: It's shut. And there'll be no one here.

ANIMAL: I'll be here, because I'm the porter. Christian Fundamentalist will be here because he trusts me. The doctor will be here because she is a doctor and everyone trusts a doctor, and you will be here, nurse, because it's your fucking job.

DEREK: But it's not my job.

ANIMAL: Tell him, doctor.

DR. LEE: We don't have — we don't have that unit — we don't have that sort of treatment — we don't have — there's nothing here.

ANIMAL: Tell 'em. Tell 'em to get it here.

DEREK: And they're going to listen. Have they ever listened? Have they, Mr Quiller?

QUILLER: They would, if Mister Bevan told 'em.

BEVAN: I — I'm just the man who's selling the hospital.

QUILLER: No, you're not. You're the man who bought the hospital.

(silence)

DR. LEE: How is your father, Quiller?

QUILLER: He's alright — well he's sort of — sort of out of it — well he's on loads of drugs and things but he's — well he don't make a lot of sense sometimes — but he's still — well he's — well he's — he's — he's dying.

DR. LEE: Quiller? Can you put that down please. (*He puts down the chainsaw.*) Doctor, porter, nurse. And Nye Bevan. Let's see what we can do, shall we?

ANIMAL: Yo.

DEREK: We can't do anything.

QUILLER: You can tell 'em. You can tell 'em they promised Doctor.

DR. LEE: We'll talk to them. Mr Bevan and I. And the paramedic will take you to pick up your father.

DEREK: I am not going anywhere.

CHRISTIAN: I thought you were.

DEREK: I mean I am not taking him anywhere.

DR. LEE: Abandoning another patient? Your medical negligence is mounting up, isn't it?

DEREK: But there's no point —

DR. LEE: And leave the medical judgement to me please.

DEREK: But —

DR. LEE: Can you just pick up my patient please? That is your job.

DEREK: Was. This is the end, the end for all of us.

DR. LEE: But I think I already knew that.

QUILLER: Dr Lee? Your name's not Jenny, is it?

DR. LEE: Funny you should say that.

QUILLER: Jenny Lee. Amazing.

DR. LEE: But it's not.

QUILLER: No. Stupid.

ANIMAL: Go on then Derek, get that siren going. And no bends at fifty.

DEREK: I'm not the driver.

ANIMAL: 'Course you're not. You're the paramedic.

(*He follows QUILLER out in a daze. QUILLER stops and turns.*)

QUILLER: You will be here?

DR. LEE: We'll be here. That's a promise.

              (*He goes.*)

CHRISTIAN: What you going to do?

DR. LEE: Tell them.

CHRISTIAN: They won't listen.

DR. LEE: I know.

BEVAN: And they won't listen to me.

DR. LEE: I know.

CHRISTIAN: So what you doing then? You can't do anything.

ANIMAL: What do you know?

CHRISTIAN: She knows. You can't, can you?

DR. LEE: No.

CHRISTIAN: So what you doing then?

DR. LEE: You're supposed to trust doctors. Well I'm a doctor Christian, and I want Quiller to trust me. That's all.

ANIMAL: Trust. Yeah.

DR. LEE: I need some morphine.

ANIMAL: Do you think that's a good idea?

DR. LEE: Not for me.

ANIMAL: Oh, right.

DR. LEE: Can you get some? A lot.

ANIMAL: Morphine. No probs.

BEVAN: Are you sure there's nothing you can give me? I'm feeling a bit stressed.

DR. LEE: I hope you're not suggesting sex, Mr Bevan.

BEVAN: Well —

ANIMAL: How about some blow? (*He gets out his stash.*)

BEVAN: Blow?

CHRISTIAN: Traditional Indian medicine.

DR. LEE: Well, as it's medicinal.

ANIMAL: Right. I'll get the morphine, you have the blow. (*tosses it to BEVAN*) Anything recreational while I'm there?

DR. LEE: Strictly medicinal.

ANIMAL: What else?

(*He goes.*)

DR. LEE: Right, Mr Bevan. We need a phone.

(*CHRISTIAN brings out a mobile.*)

CHRISTIAN: Bit of salvage.

(*DR LEE hands it to an anxious BEVAN.*)

DR. LEE: Is this your Health Service or not?

(*He takes it and dials.*)

(*GILLESPIE back at the PC.*)

GILLESPIE: You definitely do not have a stitch.

LAURA: I definitely do not have a stitch. (*The phone rings.*) I am definitely not in.

GILLESPIE: (*picking it up*) Hello — yes, but she's otherwise — Oh, Mr Bevan.

LAURA: Give it me, give it me.

GILLESPIE: Call you Nye. Right, Nye. So how is — oh I see, stress. Yes, there's a lot of it about. Dr Lee is with you?

LAURA: She's fired. Tell her, tell her.

GILLESPIE: Yes, she is a good doctor — yes, and did she have a good birthday? — she says where the fuck was I? — well —

LAURA: Mr Gillespie —

GILLESPIE: You won't be selling the hospital — well in the — not at any price — it's not for sale. (*LAURA does not look well.*) You want — sorry — you want a Chemotherapy Unit — fully staffed — right away. Yes — yes, the flower seller — yes, I do know his father — I imagine he is — you're picking him up now — you have your own ambulance. (*LAURA looks seriously unwell.*) Well — right — it might be a bit technically difficult today. Has to be before the weekend. Well look, I've got a bit of an emergency here actually. I'll have to get back to you. No, no, I will deal with it. The best way I can. Yes. Yes, I — I promise. (*puts phone down, goes over to LAURA*) Oh, Jesus Christ. (*redials*) Hello. Yes, it's an emergency. The Chief Executive's office. No, I don't require an ambulance, you bloody fool. I want a doctor, a bloody doctor, we must have one somewhere.

(*QUILLER alongside his FATHER. DEREK is bringing the stretcher in.*)

QUILLER: Dad. Dad. We're going to the hospital. We've got you a bed. A bed in the hospital. This is Derek. He's — he's a paramedic — he's going to take you there — in an ambulance. (*FATHER'S breathing is very weak and laboured.*) Dad? Dad?

DEREK: He needs help breathing. We'll give him some oxygen.

(*DEREK gets out breathing apparatus.*)

QUILLER: Derek's going to help you — help you breathe. He's a paramedic. He's good. He's been helping me.

(*DEREK puts the mask on him.*)

QUILLER: (*getting close*) Dad, I've found you a doctor, a good doctor. She's going to help you. Help you get better. She promised.

DAD: (*pushing the mask away*) I been to hospital. Didn't sell a bloody thing. That gynaecologist had a rose off me. Didn't pay. Never bloody does.

QUILLER: Dad, Dad. Mister Bevan, Nye Bevan, he came back. Came back to the hospital. The Doctor's been helping him too. He's going to tell 'em. He's going to tell 'em about the promise. Make them keep it.

DAD: Did you thank him for the beads?

QUILLER: No, I forgot. (*DEREK lifts the mask away.*) Shall we get him on?

DEREK: In a moment, Quiller.

QUILLER: Won't be long, Dad.

DAD: She a good doctor?

QUILLER: She's brilliant.

DAD: Did she pay for her roses?

QUILLER: I — I haven't given her any. But I will. Say it's from you.

DAD: Doctors are brilliant. And nurses. And porters. You can trust 'em.

QUILLER: Yeah.

DAD: Quiller. When you see Mister Bevan. When you see Nye, tell him — tell him he still owes me for the flowers.

QUILLER: What?

DAD: You tell him.

QUILLER: I don't —

DAD: He didn't pay me, did he? Bastard. Said he didn't have any money. Tell him, tell him he still owes me. But tell him, it's alright, he can have them on me. All part of the service. Tell him, Quiller. When you see Mister Bevan.

(He drifts away.)

QUILLER: Yeah, yeah, I will. *(He looks at him.)* We're part of the service, see Derek. Same as you.

DEREK: Yeah. Of course.

QUILLER: Shall we take him now?

DEREK: No. No, I don't think so, Quiller.

QUILLER: But they're waiting. The doctor's waiting.

DEREK: He's gone, Quiller.

QUILLER: But we've got to take him. The doctor's waiting. I don't want to let her down.

DEREK: You haven't let anyone down, Quiller.

(QUILLER looks at his father for a long time.)

QUILLER: We're still taking him.

DEREK: But, Quiller —

QUILLER: I promised, so we're still taking him, alright. Alright? Or do I have to take him there myself?

DEREK: No, no, 'course you don't. We'll do whatever you want.

(They move him onto the stretcher.)

QUILLER: I've got a doctor, two porters, Nye Bevan and a paramedic. I know what's what.

DEREK: You're the flower seller.

(LAURA is on the floor being attended to by a doctor. GILLESPIE is on the phone looking across at the hospital.)

DOCTOR: How long has she been like this?

GILLESPIE: She's been having attacks all morning. Asthma. (*into phone*) Yes, hello, Chief Executive's office.

LAURA: I'm alright, I'm perfectly — Gillespie, can you get this woman out of my office?

DOCTOR: Alright Laura, take it easy. Why didn't you call me before?

LAURA: I do not need you and, no, you cannot call me Laura.

GILLESPIE: She thought it was asthma. (*into phone*) Yes, that's right, chemotherapy. (*to DOCTOR*) Or a stitch.

DOCTOR: People and their bodies, they're like strangers.

LAURA: This is my body and I'd like you —

DOCTOR: I think I'd like you to relax, Laura.

LAURA: I can't recall saying you could call me Laura.

DOCTOR: I can't recall you saying anything to me.

LAURA: Gillespie.

GILLLESPIE: (*into phone*) Yes, chemotherapy — a Mr Quiller — yes, this is an executive decision.

LAURA: Gillespie.

DOCTOR: Mr Gillespie, can you get some nurses and a stretcher up here please? Right away.

LAURA: You think you know it all, don't you?

DOCTOR: No, far from it, but I do know you are quite ill Laura, and you really must calm down.

LAURA: Looking down your nose at everyone —

DOCTOR: I'm just trying to look after you —

LAURA: No, no you're not, you're not going to treat me like one of your patients.

DOCTOR: Laura, you must listen to me.

LAURA: No. I want you out of here.

DOCTOR: You've had a series of heart attacks.

LAURA: Rubbish, rubbish. Gillespie, get her out.

DOCTOR: You're liable to bring on another one, you must try and —

LAURA: Don't tell me what I've had. You're not the only one with a degree.

DOCTOR: No, I know.

LAURA: You don't know anything. You don't even know what I do.

DOCTOR: I know exactly what you —

LAURA: Tell her, Gillespie. Tell the stupid bitch what I do.

GILLESPIE: They're on their way.

DOCTOR: OK Laura, soon have you out of here.

LAURA: I'm not going anywhere.

DOCTOR: Mr Gillespie, can you —

GILLESPIE: I think you should listen to the doctor —

LAURA: No.

DOCTOR: Laura, please —

LAURA: You're not taking me out of here — I don't trust any of you — you're not touching me — you're not laying a finger — tell them, Gillespie — tell them to leave me alone — tell them what I do — just tell them — they all think they know but they don't — tell 'em, Gillespie, tell 'em. (*She goes into a deep seizure.*)

GILLESPIE: Is she alright?

DOCTOR: She won't be if they don't get a move on. Where the hell is that nurse?

GILLESPIE: I don't know what to tell them. I'm sorry I just don't know what to say.

(*Two nurses and a stretcher come in.*)

(*BEVAN, CHRISTIAN and DR LEE are sharing a spliff.*)

BEVAN: It was a piece of piss. An absolute piece of piss. I just told him what we wanted. ASAP. None of this after the weekend nonsense. I said we want it now. Easy. Like ordering from MFI.

CHRISTIAN: I hope we don't have to put it together ourselves.

BEVAN: No, because there'll be two little screws and a rawl plug left over, won't there?

CHRISTIAN: Always are.

BEVAN: No, I said I wanted staff. So they'll be with it. And one of those little trolleys to help them get it up the steps.

CHRISTIAN: I bet it doesn't have a plug.

BEVAN: Or no batteries.

CHRISTIAN: I hope it comes in a box.

BEVAN: We can play with that when they've got the unit out.

CHRISTIAN: Yeah, like when you were a kid. The washing machine boxes were really wicked.

BEVAN: Make holes in it and pretend it was your castle.

CHRISTIAN: I thought you would have made it a house with you being an estate agent.

BEVAN: I wasn't then though, was I? Not when I was eight.

CHRISTIAN: No.

BEVAN: I'm in the wrong job anyway.

DR. LEE: Where is Animal with that morphine?

CHRISTIAN: He'll be here. You can rely on Animal, he'll do anything for anyone.

BEVAN: He should be a nurse. Or a porter.

CHRISTIAN: Well he is, isn't he? We all are, aren't we? In the Health Service.

BEVAN: For today.

DR. LEE: Yeah. For today.

(*sound of the ambulance arriving*)

CHRISTIAN: Here he is. Do-or-die Derek.

BEVAN: I better put this out.

CHRISTIAN: How you feeling?

BEVAN: Sick.

DR. LEE: Lucky you're in a hospital.

(*Lights on QUILLER in front of the hospital. DEREK is bringing the stretcher.*)

QUILLER: Mister Bevan. Mister Bevan.

(*The three of them come out. They see the stretcher. DR LEE goes across to the body. DEREK shakes his head.*)

QUILLER: Hello, Mister Bevan.

BEVAN: Hello, Quiller.

QUILLER: How you feeling?

BEVAN: I'm — I'm much better.

QUILLER: Good. That's good. My father — my father had a message for you.

BEVAN: For me?

QUILLER: Yeah, he said, you still owe him for the flowers.
           Remember? You had flowers from him, on these
           steps. You didn't pay him. Hardly anyone paid
           him. Patients, doctors, nurses — he used to give
           nearly everything away. Said it was part of the
           service. He wanted to be part of the service. But
           he wasn't, was he? He wasn't paid. And you
           didn't pay him, Mister Bevan. So you still owe
           him for the flowers.

           (*BEVAN vainly searches his pyjamas.*)

BEVAN: I don't have any money, Quiller.

QUILLER: You don't have any money. Do you hear that
           Dad, he doesn't have any money. Why do they
           never have any fucking money?

BEVAN: Christian —

QUILLER: No worries, Mister Bevan. My father says it's
           alright, you can have them on him.

DR. LEE: I'm really sorry, Quiller.

QUILLER: You don't have to be sorry. Not you. You're a
           doctor. (*He gives her a flower.*) You buggers never
           pay, he said. He wouldn't let you. (*He picks up two
           cans of paint stripper left by the salvage team. He
           turns to Christian.*) For the flowers.

CHRISTIAN: Yeah. For the flowers.

           (*QUILLER goes to the hospital front and starts to
           empty the cans, dousing a trail inside.*)

CHRISTIAN: What's he doing?

DR. LEE: Whatever he wants.

           (*ANIMAL arrives.*)

ANIMAL: Sorry, really sorry I'm late.

DR. LEE: You're not late Animal, you're not late at all.

ANIMAL: Shit. Shit.

(*QUILLER comes back out.*)

BEVAN: Quiller? Are you alright?

QUILLER: I'm fine, Mister Bevan. Just sorting out a memorial. Your memorial. Not the one they wanted though. Memorial's got to have flowers. Flowers at midnight. Anyone got a light?

(*They all look at each other.*)

CHRISTIAN: Yeah, sure.

(*CHRISTIAN hands QUILLER the lighter. QUIL-LER bends down, ignites the trail.*)

(*LAURA is on the stretcher, complete with oxygen mask. GILLESPIE is looking out of the window.*)

GILLESPIE: Jesus Christ.

(*The DOCTOR joins him.*)

DOCTOR: Someone's having a party.

GILLESPIE: Yeah. Yeah, I bet they are. (*They start to wheel LAURA away.*)

DOCTOR: Heart's the last thing we think of, you know? Think of everything else from hormone replacement to colon irrigation. But the poor old heart, we forget it's there. Until it's too late.

GILLESPIE: Yeah, that's true. (*He is still looking out of the window.*)

DOCTOR: They're going to have a job putting that out.

GILLESPIE: Yeah. Definitely.

(*The stretcher has gone. The DOCTOR follows. GILLESPIE remains watching.*)

(QUILLER is sitting by the stretcher. They are all facing the hospital, saying nothing. MENDLESON arrives.)

MEN.: Holy Moses. Look at that. What a waste. What an absolute waste. *(They barely look at him.)* All those artefacts going up in smoke. They'll be a bit of compensation here. *(ANIMAL gives him a glare.)* Well, it's not just money. It's a legacy. There could have been bits of this hospital all over the country to remember it by.

ANIMAL: You really are a clueless tosser, aren't you?

MEN.: Eh, do you want to keep your job?

ANIMAL: No. I want you to stuff your job.

MEN.: Don't turn your nose up at it. I'm talking about work of real value. Real value. But I don't suppose you know what that means, do you?

CHRISTIAN: Yeah, we do.

MEN.: Oh, do you?

DR. LEE: Yes, they do Mr Mendleson.

DEREK: Yeah.

BEVAN: Yes. They do.

QUILLER: They all do.

ANIMAL: See. That's a reference from a doctor, a paramedic, a flower seller and Nye Bevan. You can't get better than that.

QUILLER: No. You can't.

(CHRISTIAN switches on the ghetto blaster. We hear 'Design for Life'.)

End

About the Author

Laurence Allan was born in Pontypridd and went to Pontypridd Boys' Grammar School, which he deserted when he was sixteen. He then worked as a meter reader, a banana packer and on the legendary Ponty Market before leaving the town to train as a teacher in Manchester.

Leaving there in 1975 he discovered a thin talent as an actor which he managed to stretch over the next ten years throughout a host of dying English theatres. In London in 1984 during the Miners strike he discovered the need to write and returned to Wales that year to produce his own play, a celebration of striking miners' wives, *Over the Wall and Back Again*, which toured around the South Wales Valleys.

He became one of Made in Wales' school of writers making his mark with *A Blow to Bute Street* at the Sherman Theatre, Cardiff and has gone on to have close to twenty plays produced.

His radio plays include *Cries Across the Tracks* and *I Was a Teenage Playboy* and he is one of the original writers of the Radio Wales daily drama, *Station Road*.

He has one television credit to date, *Rainbow Chaser*, and is currently working on the forthcoming BBC TV spin-off of *Station Road*. He has recently finished writing a film of *King of the Mountains* which is in commission with the BBC.